GOD OR CHAOS

GOD OR CHAOS

BY

REV. ROBERT KANE, S.J.

NEW YORK
P. J. KENEDY & SONS
PRINTERS TO THE HOLY APOSTOLIC SEE

Imprimi Potest

JOSEPH BROWNE, S.J.
Provincial, England

Nihil Obstat

REV. REMY LAFORT, D.D.
Censor Librorum

Imprimatur

☩ JOHN CARDINAL FARLEY
Archbishop of New York
NEW YORK
October 22, 1912

TO

THE RIGHT HONOURABLE

CHRISTOPHER PALLES, LL.D.

OF HIS MAJESTY'S PRIVY COUNCILS

OF IRELAND AND ENGLAND

LORD CHIEF BARON OF THE

EXCHEQUER

BY SPECIAL PERMISSION

AND WITH AFFECTIONATE ESTEEM

ROBERT KANE, S.J.

Milltown Park, Dublin,
Whit Sunday, 1912.

MY DEAR CHIEF BARON, — *There are many reasons why I*
should ask your permission to dedicate this Book to you.   Your
keen and subtle sense of logic, your broad and balanced judg-
ment, your profound knowledge of Law, and your wide and
varied knowledge of many subjects outside your own profes-
sion, — these are assuredly reasons why I should esteem it an
honour to have this Work on Fundamental Philosophy associ-
ated with your name.   But, there is a still more potent motive
in my ambition to claim this privilege.   Your strong yet gentle
character, your uncompromising loyalty to Truth yet large-
minded appreciation of the views of others, your convinced yet
childlike reverence for Religion, your cheerful kindliness towards
all, your staunch faithfulness towards your friends, your blame-
less career and your devout life, are titles to an admiration which
no wisdom could call forth, nor any knowledge command.   Fur-
thermore, there are many bonds of sympathy between us; amongst
them, our fond allegiance to our dear old Alma Mater, Clon-
gowes Wood College, and, above all, an unfailing personal friend-
ship of more than thirty years.   There is yet another reason.
It is an incident in appearance trifling, but in fact to me of
supreme importance.   More than twenty years ago I lent you
this Book in order to have your opinion of it.   Meeting me
some short while afterwards, you said to me: "Your Book is
very deep.   It is very hard reading.   I fear that you will find

very few to understand it." Some time elapsed before I met you again. On this occasion you said: *"I have been looking through your Book again, and this time at greater leisure I have quite changed my opinion. When one reads it slowly and thought-fully, it is very simple. Any ordinary person who gives the time and takes the trouble, ought to be able to understand it all."* It is fitting that to you, from whom this Book received its first word of encouragement, should be offered the first tribute of its publication.

I am, my dear Chief Baron,

Your old and attached friend,

ROBERT KANE, S.J.

PREFACE

THE subject-matter of this work presents a double difficulty. It demands deep and tough thinking. It needs clear and precise expression. This double difficulty is intensified in our day. Our age is in such fever haste that it is impatient of deep reasoning which must be slow, while it will snatch up any appearance of proof which it may find upon the surface. It is so conceited that it arrogantly challenges all truth which it does not understand, while it contemptuously refuses the time and trouble necessary for the understanding of it. It is so prejudiced that it is docile or even credulous in matters of mere material knowledge, while it is defiant or even cynical towards abstract thoughtfulness. It is so radical that it is as rebel against the laws of language as against the authority of kings. But if ever age had need of understanding the reason of God, it is our own.

This Book was written more than twenty-five years ago. It is the fruit of long years of patient meditation and of strenuous study. It has been matured while the writer was teaching the matter of it to able and mature minds. Ever since it has been waiting for the calm judgment of experience.

As to my method, I should wrathfully disdain to seek, even were this possible, to bully other minds by bludgeon blows of dogmatism or to entrap them with artifice of oratory. My aim is to conquer only, if at all, by point of proof and edge of argument.

My emphatic and unhesitating way of speaking does not come from any overweening trust in my own powers, but from an absolute conviction of the truth to which I owe and render a frank and fearless allegiance. With the thorough consciousness which I have of the divine fulness and efficacy of my cause, it is scarcely possible that I should not speak like a soldier on the battlefield, whose sword is unsheathed and who knows that the victory is on his side.

Yet, after all, this thought comes back to me, that the truth is safe, while the wandering searchers after truth are not safe; and therefore I should like to rewrite much of what I have written, lest perchance some angry or harsh word of mine should wound some honest seeker. But I cannot now do so. Maimed as I am my work must remain as it is.

I do hope that any earnest worshipper of God who reads this Book may find therein something to strengthen and comfort him. I do pray that any open-minded Atheist who comes across these pages may find, however harshly he judge of the writer, something in what is written that will enable him to win his way to the home of the loving Father of

all.   Should I become the means of reflecting God's
sunshine to but one soul that sitteth in darkness,
I shall have received, in overflowing measure, the
most desired mead of recompense for all my toil.

ROBERT KANE, S.J.

WHIT SUNDAY, 1912.

CONTENTS

First Book

REALITIES AND REASONS

CHAPTER I. ARISTOTLE IN PLAIN CLOTHES

PAGE

Section 1. A matter of fact man. 3
2. A philosopher 6
3. Philosophy in plain words 8

CHAPTER II. BEGINNINGS

Section 1. Why we must begin 11
2. Clearing the ground 14
3. The starting-point 16

CHAPTER III. POSSIBILITY

Section 1. What Possibility does not mean 29
2. What Possibility does mean 31
3. The reason of Possibility 33

CHAPTER IV. REALITY

Section 1. Realised Fact 36
2. Realised Truth 42
3. Realised Conditions 44

CHAPTER V. THE FIRST REALITY OF FACTS AND THE FINAL TRUTH OF REASONS

Section 1. Facts that are not First and Reasons that are not Final 46
2. Can the Universe exist as a Mutual Aid Society? . . 50
3. A First Fact that is Final Truth 58

CONTENTS

CHAPTER VI. IS THERE A GOD?

PAGE

Section 1. Atheists and Agnostics 61
       2. Mental attitudes towards Truth 76
       3. Meaning of the Question 84

Second Book

"I AM WHO AM"

PAGE

PROOF I. The existence of Contingent Facts is a realised proof of the existence of a Necessary Being 93

PROOF II. The Principle of Causality proves the Existence of God 103

PROOF III. The existence of Potential and Determinable Realities proves the existence of a Being that is simply and solely active 110

PROOF IV. The Possibility of Self-existent Being proves its Actual Existence 113

PROOF V. The Possibility of Anything proves the Existence of God 120

PROOF VI. The Existence of God is proved from the objective standard and rule of judgment 125

PROOF VII. The Existence of God is proved by the Subjective nature of Will 133

PROOF VIII. The actual existence of positive and different degrees of perfection proves the actual Existence of God . . 143

PROOF IX. The Law of Conscience proves the Existence of God 152

PROOF X. The Order existing in the Universe proves the Existence of God 163

PROOF XI. Human reason has declared that God exists . . 176

PROOF XII. Without God, there is left Chaos 186

CONTENTS

Third Book

THE NATURE OF NECESSARY BEING

CHAP.   PAGE

   I. THE ESSENCE OF NECESSARY BEING 193

  II. THE INFINITY OF NECESSARY BEING 196

 III. UNITY OF NECESSARY BEING 198

 IV. ETERNITY OF NECESSARY BEING 200

  V. PERSONALITY OF NECESSARY BEING 205

 VI. KNOWLEDGE OF GOD 210

VII. WILL OF NECESSARY BEING 213

VIII. POWER OF GOD 215

Fourth Book

A TRIPLE TOUCHSTONE

CHAP.   PAGE

   I. FREE-WILL 219

  II. THE ORIGIN OF EVIL 227

 III. HELL 232

 IV. FAITH 239

CONCLUSION 242

First Book

REALITIES AND REASONS

GOD OR CHAOS

𝔉𝔦𝔯𝔰𝔱 𝔅𝔬𝔬𝔨

CHAPTER I

ARISTOTLE IN PLAIN CLOTHES

SECTION I. A MATTER-OF-FACT MAN

THERE is no sane person who does not know something.
Sensible men claim to have a fair share of plain practical
knowledge. Now, when we carefully sift what people
say, we always find in the end some grains of conviction
that are thoroughly pure and absolutely honest. Again,
when we remove all the dross that can have gathered,
owing to particular causes or individual accidents, the
sterling stuff which forms the inmost core of human
judgments is of exactly the same kind in all. All practical people consider themselves perfectly secure from
error and perfectly safe in argument if they can take
shelter behind certain stout facts and stand upon certain
unshakable principles. It is to the same facts and to
the same principles that all men make their ultimate
appeal. There are some few truths which ordinary folk
look on as absolutely undeniable. Men simply cannot
believe that any one in his senses does really doubt
them.

Should a respectable citizen, under an intense strain
of mental depression, commit murder and attempt

suicide, the Jury will find a verdict of "temporary insanity." So, when a clever writer is unnerved and overwrought by such morbid doubts and logical worries, as, in a paroxysm of intellectual tangle, to deny his own knowledge of his own existence, the general public will pity rather than blame him, and they will charitably say that he is "an eccentric genius."

Now, whether it is wiser to regulate one's thought by these intellectual meteors or to follow the movement of uniform and universal consent, is at present no concern of mine. I merely call attention to this fact, that there are some truths about which all men practically are so simply and absolutely agreed as to be unable to understand any denial or doubt of them. What these particular truths are is a further question. We get nearer and nearer to them according as we relentlessly set aside all assertions that are not immediate, certain, evident judgments of reason. When we have put apart whatever can be accounted for by fancy, prejudice, interest, or other outside cause, there is left only that which comes straight out from the very nature of reason itself. Now, what comes from reason itself is common to all reasonable men, and therefore the unadulterated sense of mankind is called our common-sense. Thus common-sense has two relative meanings which imply and complete each other, that of the body of truths which all men hold, and that of man's rational faculty in so far as this, in all men, judges in the same simple, natural, spontaneous, inevitable, downright and irreconcilable way. Hence, a decision of common-sense is the unanimous unmistakable and unmistaken verdict of reasonable men.

The most fundamental ground of common-sense is that reasonable men have a reason for what they think.

They must have a reason why they know what they do know. They may not be able to explain themselves thoroughly. A reasonable man may not even be always able to give a reason for his conviction. But, common-sense at least lays down that a conviction for which there is no reason is unreasonable. When men really believe a fact, it is either because this fact has been sufficiently brought under their own actual experience, or because it has been made known to them by what they reasonably take as reasonably sufficient proof. When men reasonably hold to a principle, it is either because there is sufficiently evident reason in it for its own acceptance, or because there is sufficient reason to support it in the evidence of some underlying truth.

But, that a man should admit facts or adopt principles without sufficient reason, is, if he does not know what he is doing, a logical mistake; if he does know it, a logical misdemeanour. On the other hand, if a man unwittingly denies what is shown to have sufficient reason, he is, in so far forth, a fool. If he wilfully deny it, he is a knave.

Now, all this, namely, that knowledge implies a sufficient reason for what is known, rests upon this other and still more fundamental ground, that there is a real reason why things are what they are. For, truth is only the likeness of things and what is right in logic presupposes what is real in fact. In other words, nothing is known unless it be knowable, and nothing is knowable unless it have reason enough in itself to render reasonable the thought that thinks it.

Common-sense is very reasonable. It is also very safe and very shrewd. It won't say Yea or Nay without sufficient reason. Common-sense is too honest to sin against the light, or to proclaim that there can be only darkness in the day, when as yet it sees no more than dawn. It is too honourable to put fancy for fact, or to push doubt into denial. Common-sense has one fixed point which is the fulcrum of all its force, one cardinal principle on which all its action, one way or the other, towards affirmation or towards negation, hinges. All things that are real, and all truths that are reasonable, have a sufficient reason why they are so. If your ideas about this are still hazy, just think it out and talk it over with some hard-headed matter-of-fact man.

SECTION 2. A PHILOSOPHER

A philosopher is a reasoner. What he looks for in all things is truth, and what he looks for in all truth is the why and the wherefore of it. Not only will he take nothing merely on trust, but even when you bring him face to face with an undeniable fact, he will still want to understand it. He is not satisfied even when you give him a good reason. He must have a good reason for that reason, he will not stop reasoning until he has got to a reason which is fully and finally sufficient.

Thus, while a plain man is quite content to ground his life on near facts which he knows to be real, and to guide his life by near principles which he knows to be true, a philosopher will only begin with first facts and only end with final reasons. All men who reason out things are in so far forth philosophers. A thorough philosopher is a man who reasons out everything, and reasons it out thoroughly. Hence, with regard to what they know, there is only a difference of degree between a philosopher and a plain man. The one reasons from point to point, the other reasons from end to end. In as far as he really reasons, each is a reasonable man. Hence, however high a philosopher may sometimes soar above the understanding of ordinary men, he will, unless he should have gone astray, come back from his flights to their home of solid common-sense. Wherefore, with regard to what he knows, a philosopher is simply a reasoner who follows truth up and down the whole scale of evidence, gauging the height and depth of principles, measuring the force of proof and the area of Conclusion, estimating the action and reaction of relative Certainties, recognising the perspective of interdependent realities, so that the fundamental causes which, with mutual clasp, bind all things into one universe, are reflected in the thinking of his thought, and mirrored forth in one supreme and systematic wisdom.

But, it is the way in which he knows things that marks off the philosopher from out of the rest of reasonable men. He not only knows what he knows, but he knows why he knows it, how he knows it, what bearing this knowledge has on whatever else he knows, as well as where, why and how his knowledge grows dim, hesitating or hazardous, and where, why and how it at last stops short.

Wherefore, a philosopher is a reasoner who reasons out both the reasons and the reasoning of his knowledge. He is a reasoner both in his direct understanding of things, in his rational method of reaching them, in his comprehensive hold of them, and also in his conscious starting from the absolute evidence of primal principles, in his thorough insight into the reasonableness of his own steps, in his supreme intellectual ownership of his own reason and of his own reasoning. As one fails to attempt this, one is a plain man. As one fails to accomplish it, one is a poor philosopher. Thus, after all, Philosophy is nothing more than common-sense brought to scientific perfection. A philosopher is, then, a thorough and scientific reasoner.

But, again, a reasoner is not satisfied to know facts. He further wants to know the reasons for them. A thorough reasoner wants to know the reasons that are full and final. Thus, again, all Philosophy is the outcome of that necessity which mind has in knowledge, as reality has in fact, of having a sufficient reason for thought or thing.

SECTION 3. PHILOSOPHY IN PLAIN WORDS

In one sense, Philosophy is the simplest thing in the world. It is the natural and immediate object of that reason which is common to all men. It only requires that reason be used in the most reasonable manner. It does not need any store of facts to start with, nor any wealth of information to pay its way. It lives and thrives on such knowledge as is universal as the air. It is independent of laboratories, instruments, or equipments. It consists merely in the most reasonable use of reason.

In another sense, Philosophy is the most difficult of all sciences. It dwells in the region of the most abstract and rarified thought. It walks where the swerve of a hair-breadth means a fall into fundamental error. It works with principles which are of absolute delicacy and of absolute danger. Its output must be of almost infinitesimal nicety, and of almost infinite magnitude. Its analysis must reach to the ultimate elements of truth, and its synthesis must gather all sciences into the most perfect unity of wisdom.

Philosophy, to some extent, is inseparable from the mental action of every sane adult, for it is reason as it looks to the reasons of things. In a fairly full sense, Philosophy is possible to every sensible man, for in matters that are the common ground of all sensible men, each is capable, with time and trouble, of finding reasons that are evidently and ultimately sufficient. But in a complete sense, Philosophy needs a special taste, for all men cannot bear the strain of intense and prolonged abstraction. It needs a special training, for it is only by careful and systematic exercise that our higher logical powers are developed to mature and harmonised strength. It needs a special teaching, for the range of reason is so vast, learning so slow, the dangers of mistake so innumerable and our mental vision so feeble, that without the luminous help of the wisdom of the world as it is concentrated on our path by an experienced mind, we, ordinary folk at least, are sure to miss our way. The simplicity of Philosophy tempts many to rush headlong into its depths when they have got tired of dabbling in shallow sciences. The sublimity of Philosophy overwhelms, confuses, stuns, crushes many foolhardy people who will not reflect that Metaphysic is more deep and dangerous than the sea, and they are flung back to common life without the common certainties of commonsense.

If it is hard enough to explain the meaning of a simple term; much more must it be difficult to put simple ideas and first principles into plain words. The more fundamental a truth is, so is it more universal, and so more wide in its meaning, and so more simple in the vagueness of its thought, and so more intangible when we attempt to explain it in full yet accurate, clear yet scientific speech. The more simple an idea is, the fewer and the more indefinite are the ideas on which we can fall back in order to express, or explain it. Hence when we undertake to sift our very first notions, we must expect to encounter great difficulty in the understanding of them, since we are in the highest sphere of intellectual research and reflection. We must expect to encounter still greater difficulty in the utterance of them, since we would represent the finest and most abstract shades of thought through the cumbersome and most concrete medium of language. Philosophers, like other scientists, have their own short and pithy formulas, but their terseness is not clear to outsiders. Again, many words hide rather than clothe truth. Thus, whatever road we take, in our Philosophy, we must be ready for real, downright, hard thinking. Without downright hard thinking, there can be no deep Philosophy. We will aim at being thorough, and yet, as far as may be, clear. We do not ambition that clearness which is only got by shirking tough brain-work, but we do strive after that clearness which consists in the use of plain words. No Philosopher will read these Chapters without finding matter for serious reflection, and yet we think that there will be very few words to be met with in them likely to puzzle the wits of even a plain man. We must reach the most sublime truths, but we want to get up to them by the easiest and simplest paths.

CHAPTER II

BEGINNINGS

SECTION I.   WHY WE MUST BEGIN

In order to set about thinking, we must start from some point or other.   In this sense, if we do not begin to think, we do not think at all.   But, must we begin in a strict sense?   Must we begin from the beginning?   Is there a real beginning in Philosophy, from which if we do not begin, we simply cannot get to any Philosophy? Is there a principle or system of principles, so foremost and so fundamental, as to be, in logical order and in real importance, of all necessity, first?

There are derived and dependent principles.

Therefore, there are first principles. A second is impossible unless there be a first. The truth of this will be more telling if we shut out a meaning that might cause mistake.

A railway carriage cannot be the second one of a train unless there is another between it and the locomotive. But should the station-master wish to do so, he can have that particular carriage put first.   Thus, if it is second, we must infer that there is a first.   But, we cannot argue from the existence of that carriage that there must be another before it.   In other words, as the position of a carriage in a train is quite accidental to its nature, we cannot, from the existence of such outside relation, conclude that it is a relation which is necessary.

It is quite another matter when the order between first and second neither comes from chance nor yields to change, but clings to their very kind.

The wheels of a steam-engine are moved by a lever. The lever is moved by a piston. The piston is moved by the steam. The steam is generated by the action of heat upon water. Here, we have a sequence which is necessary, not merely accidental. If you upset this order, you destroy the steam-engine.

In a string of assertions, may be met with one or other of these two sorts of sequence. There is rarely more than an accidental connection between the questions asked by members in Parliament, or between the answers given by vendors of purloined articles, or between the sentences huddled together in after-dinner speeches. But, among logical principles, there is a hierarchy of truth the order of which is absolutely essential. A truth which is not primary, essentially includes, and therefore logically presupposes, some truth that is simpler than itself. Thus, this principle "A man must do his duty" presupposes that he has duties. This presupposes that he can have duties. This presupposes that he can be under a moral obligation. This presupposes that he can be bound by a force which is not physical but moral. This presupposes that he is able either wrongfully to neglect or rightfully to fulfil his duty. This presupposes that, while he is not able to do both at the same time because they are contrary one to the other, yet he is at the same time able to do both because both at once are in his power. This presupposes that he is free. This presupposes that he is intelligent. This presupposes that he exists. This presupposes that he is possible. This presupposes that something is possible. This presupposes that there is a difference between what is and what is not. This presupposes that everything is not nothing.

Men who suit their Philosophy to their taste, or who shape it to the measure of their practice, are like the preacher who admired how Nature had set great rivers near big cities. Men who look for a Philosophy without first principles are like children who should fancy that the wheels of a steam-engine could be coaxed into running round without the piston, or that the piston could be persuaded to rush up and down without the steam.

Philosophy must begin somewhere: firstly, because the more perfect and scientific reasoning is, the more thoroughly should it be able to show that it is quite at one with common-sense, and this implies that it has set forth from, and can therefore go back to, reason's A. B. C: secondly, because a reasoner who does not begin from first principles can do no more than build castles in the air, for he has no solid ground underneath his system: thirdly, because the whole object, duty, and privilege of Philosophy are in the giving of rational proof. Now, rational proof consists in the turning towards some higher principle from which the proven principle borrows light. But, if there are no ultimate truths that are evident with the simple shining of their own light, there is, ultimately, no light to be borrowed and therefore no proof to be got. Hence, a Philosophy without first principles is light without source, leverage without fixity, movement without direction, reasoning without reason. Proof points to a previous principle. It is not, then, upon proof but upon evidence, that Philosophy must ultimately rest. From first principles therefore, must Philosophy begin.

SECTION 2.   CLEARING THE GROUND

There are many men who overestimate their own mental power. If they have a good manner, they are often taken by others, not according to their real worth, but at the price which they put upon themselves. Deference, or even politeness makes them grow aggressive. They become intellectual bullies. One phase of their character is that of positive and peremptory dictation. They are addicted to excessive affirmation. Not to be at once convinced of all that they say, is to forfeit their friendship. But, if hard pressed by a stubborn assailant in argument, they drop their logical weapons, and try to sanction their statements by devout appeals to commonsense. This implied claim to a monopoly of commonsense, if hidden under a sparkling grace of style or happy gift of speech, is frequently successful with the crowd.

Yet, excess in affirmation is not the fault typical of our times. This is rather excess in negation. It calls itself a critical spirit. Now this critical spirit is even more tyrannical than the other, and far more vehement in its dogmatism. It is so easy to deny, so hard to prove; so simple to doubt, so troublesome to be wise; so defiant to have no faith, and so vulgar to cling to an old creed, that a boy with a little smartness and a little learning, can enjoy the luxury of professing to be sure of nothing. This kind of dogmatism is imposed upon the credulous by means of a covert assumption of scientific insight, recommended by an open and very tragic avowal of ignorance.

In both cases, authority is pushed to despotism. It is sought to hypnotise us into the surrender of our own reason by the magnetic murmuring of some great name.

When we sturdily resist, we are held as proven guilty of arrogating to ourselves more weight and wisdom than we allow to the demigod before whose unproven infallibility we will not bow. This is unfair, because a fool may be sometimes wise just where a wise man is a fool. It is unsafe, because, as the strongest force does most damage when loosened from its proper sphere, so the mightiest minds blunder most woefully when they meddle with what they do not know.

Philosophy is all reasoning and only reasoning. Philosophy is the intellectual seeing of things in themselves. If it take anything whatsoever upon trust, it is not Philosophy at all: It is Faith. Authority, if accredited by reason, may, even in Philosophy, point out the right road. But a Philosopher cannot do his own walking by proxy. However reasonable or necessary Faith may be, it is not sight. Now, Philosophy may be weak, short, dim, but as far as it goes, it is sight. We may, then, act upon a true man's word, and believe when we cannot see; but, we cannot think with another man's brain nor become philosophers by holding to the skirts of Comte, Kant, or Aristotle.

Wherefore, our intellectual aristocrats, with their pretty wreaths, sparkling coronets, or rich robes, will do for lookers-on around the arena of Philosophy. We will give them all the applause they want in Literature, in Science, or in Art. But, if they wish to win here, they must step down from their high places, doff their fine clothes, step forward into the ring on equal footing with ourselves, and be ready for a rough and most undignified tumble in the dust, unless, with the thews and sinews of reason, they can prove themselves to be the better men.

What about common-sense? We must, first of all, identify it. There is a vast amount of adulterated stuff passed off by pushing retailers of learning under the brand of common-sense, while there is a great deal of genuine truth slurred over sneeringly by amateurs whose science consists in "the groundless denial of all that seems to them groundlessly asserted." Now, common-sense can only be identified by the evidence of its own reasoning, or by the proof of its reasonable parentage. Hence, we can accept no statement, no doubt, no denial, unless it give a reason for itself. Everything has a reason, and, as long as there is a reason to give, a reasoner must be ready to give it. Where proof is possible, a philosopher must have proof. Where proof is impossible, this will be either because the matter appears to be merged in darkness, in which case the philosopher will wait silently looking for the dawn; or it will be because the matter is itself a very source of evidence, in which case, as there is a dimness in the eye, not a spot upon the sun, it is not proof but explanation which must clear the mind to see the light.

Wherefore, as we must begin from the beginning, we thrust aside everything about which reasonable men, in their calm and meditative moments, do really doubt. We build only upon such principles as can, to reasonable men, be made plain by proof, if they be not already evident from mere explanation.

SECTION 3.   THE STARTING-POINT

Although, in practical life everybody admits the reality of many facts and the truth of many principles, yet, in philosophic thought, as we must explain or prove each fact or principle, we must work our way back to first facts and work our way on to reasons that are final. This does not imply any quarrel with common-sense. It means that common-sense, which usually looks only outward from itself and at the outside kind of things, should try to reach the inward understanding both of itself and of whatever else it knows.

First, we must find our fixed point in the world of fact. To stop short at a fact because it is a fact, and to say that there is nothing more to be said about it, is often the only sensible thing to do in the business or pleasure of our daily lives. But, in the following up of argument or in the unfolding of theory, no man will be satisfied with woman's reason. "It is, because it is." There is an infinite region beyond my own consciousness. But, all that is ideal need not be actual. How can I distinguish between fact and phantom? How can I come in touch with the reality that is outside myself? Were my intellect able to behold, with direct and immediate intuition, the innermost reality of things I should not need sight in order to recognise a presence, nor hearing in order to catch a sound. For, in that case, mind, without let or hindrance from matter, would pierce through outward show or surface-semblance, and penetrate, with unveiled gaze, to the naked identity whereby substance is its own self. But, since our mind does not reach to facts except through their appearances we can only test the reality of a thing by the reality of its evident showing to ourselves. Yet, again, whether this showing of thing to thought, this mental realisation of what is outside the mind, be empty fancy or downright fact, dream or truth; whether it be only an inevitable judgment behind which we cannot get, or at most a logical phase of ideal existence, all this I can decide only by reason of the knowledge that I am myself a fact. Thus, the ground on which all my fact-knowledge must rest is the consciousness that I myself exist. The fact of my own existence is the one point where all my knowledge of reality begins. Without the knowledge of this fact, the real cannot be distinguished from the ideal, nor can we know whether indeed what is, be more than what merely seems to be.

Mark however, that it is not quite our bare existence, as a substance, which is directly manifest to us. Rather, it is the solid, practical, concrete fact of actual thought or wish, of feeling or of deed which stirs and lights up my consciousness with the thrilling evidence of my thinking, wishing, feeling, acting, self.

That this fact cannot be proved would undermine all our knowledge of reality, if it were a doubtful fact or one that needed proof. But, after all, proof only gives second-hand truth. Evidence gives truth first-hand. This evident, undeniable, unmistakable, living reality of one's own existence is the first fact in Philosophy.

We have now to find a first fixed point in the region of abstract truth. As truths approach more closely to concrete fact, so are they more full of affirmation. But this, while it makes them more complex, makes them also less wide in their application, and less deep in their importance. Thus, a truth that is nearly akin to practice is formed as it were of successive strata of assertions, each of which presupposes and adds to those that had been laid down before. Hence in order to reason out such a proposition, we must remove one layer after another, until we have got to some primeval evidence. But as we are getting deeper, we are leaving aside peculiar

and occasional results, and, in like measure, we are
reaching to logical foundations more and more solid
because more primal, more and more far-spread because
more simple, more and more absolute because more
universal. Wherefore in Philosophy, we resolve arguments into their elements, we unravel reasons into their
strands, we fuse truths into their principles.

A principle is what is head, chief, source, or origin.

A logical principle is a fountain-truth both in that
its own evidence springs forth from it, and in that from
it flows proof for derived conclusions. But, even among
principles there must be order. There cannot be a
relation of antagonism among truths. For, the implaca-
ble rigour of Logic annihilates utterly all real opposition.
Therefore, there must exist at least the relation of
alliance. Yet, again alliance on a footing of equality
would render them independent of each other.

But, independence among logical principles would
break through the supreme necessity of their union.
Nay; there is need of even more than union among them.
There must be unity. The essential oneness of Logic
involves the absolute empire of truth, and this involves
some sort of subordination even among logical principles.

Now, since truth is only the intellectual reflection of
thing, our First Principle must be the affirmation of
what in Being is first and most fundamental. That such
a principle presupposes none other and is itself pre-
supposed to all, follows from its logical identity with
the notion of Being, as this is the kernel of every affirmation and of every negation.

Now, there is nothing prior in Being to its own identity
with itself. The truth of it may be expressed thus;
"Whatever is, is." Its negative aspect may be put;

"Whatever is, is not nothing." Both its positive and its negative aspects, its identity with what is itself, and its distinction from what is not itself, can be set together so as to exclude all cavil about change or likeness or relation, in this way; "One and the same thing cannot, at one and the same time, under one and the same respect, both be and not be." We may call this principle, "The Principle of Contradiction," because it affirms, in relation to reality, the absolute opposition between Being and Nothing, and, in relation to logic, the utter antagonism between truth and falsehood. Any attempt to prove this principle would be both needless and absurd, because the admission of it is implied in the very possibility of reasoning. Thus, then, the Principle of Contradiction is the point, in the ideal world, from which a philosopher must start.

One more fixed point is wanted in order to complete our system of forces. We have spoken of the First Fact and of the First Principle. We have now to speak of the First Condition. It is this; our mind can know truth. By this, we not only gain sure footing in the real and in the ideal world, we are also enabled to pass with certainty from one to the other. Here, least of all, is strict proof possible. For, proof is an appeal to reason, and an appeal to reason is an assertion of reason's competency to judge truly. But, proof, were it possible, would be utterly useless. The matter is simply and absolutely evident. If there be any truth, any evidence, any certainty, it can only be in so far forth as we can know truth, see evidence, accept certainty. We do not mean now to attack the sturdy Scotch School. They have good heads that think deeply, and, although some of them might prefer to set it in another shape, they would broadly admit all that we say. Nor, indeed, do we aim a thrust at any Philosophy that is more than fictitious. There is now no question whatever of what is, or is not, true, but merely as to whether anything is true. No reasonable man stands against this. Does it seem unfair to say so much? It is really impossible to say less. Outside the very small circle of professional philosophers, no man has any misgivings about the accuracy of mind in some matters. With regard to philosophers, whether they be trained professionals or dabbling amateurs, the overwhelming majority of them hold to the possibility of true knowledge. For, without this, Science has no credential, and Philosophy no excuse. A few wild writers flippantly deny all this, or superbly define to be inane the reasons offered in support of it. Now, this dogmatism of destruction is a savage and uproarious revolt against reason. It is besides immoral. For, it claims to dictate conclusions without any conviction, and to rule belief without any authority. If no affirmation is secure, no denial can stand. If other men cannot know what is true, much less can these men know what is false. As to those who stop short of denial, but stand in doubt, most of them are unconsciously quibbling. If they only doubt about the veracity of thought, they have no right to rail against superstition, to anathematise Theology, to deify Science, or to adore the "Age." If they do doubt, how do they know what is true, or what is false? If they do not know truth from falsehood, it seems rather reckless on their part to preach. If Agnosticism be thorough and sincere, its only duty is to be silent and its only right to learn. To say that one doubts, and at the same time to maintain that what another says is false, is not loyal.

Denial of the false is only possible by reason of one's knowledge of the true. Those, then, who profess to know nothing, cannot honestly deny Anything.

Undogmatic doubt is a frequent and an honourable phase of mind in reference to philosophic questions. All who hold to any positive opinion, whether it be a definition or a denial, do in fact assert that they know the truth, and that therefore, in their own case at least, truth is really knowable by mind. But, we may now leave them aside, and turn to those who do not dogmatise, but who are really, as they profess to be, in doubt. Let it be kept well in view that there is no question of the truth or falsehood of any particular proposition. We have only to see whether it is ever or in any case reasonable for a man to rely with absolute trust upon his own thought as a pure mirror of truth and a right representation of reality. To attempt to prove this, would be to beg the question. An explanation ought to make its evidence, which is better than any proof, visible.

Each nature works according to its kind. Each element has its own affinities. Each tree builds up its own wood. Our eyes are not fashioned to appreciate sound, but to receive impressions of colour and to react with a living image which is sight. Now, mind is representative. Whether or no there be any rhyme or reason in it, mind does think, tell, judge, intellectually see. Whether truly or falsely, it does represent. Whether from inborn tendency or from incoming influence, it must represent. That is the nature of it. It is, then, made to represent. It may, indeed, not actually represent anything; but, it never can represent nothing. Nothing is not capable of being represented. Hence, mind is made to represent something. But, what is simply unreal is simply nothing.

Therefore, mind cannot be made to represent the bare, bald absence of truth, for this is simple and utter unreality, that is to say, simple and utter nothing. Neither can the nature of mind be to represent what is false. What is false can only be represented by a faculty made to represent what is true. Look well to this point.

Truth, in its moral meaning, is the conformity of outward sign or speech to what is in the mind. Truth, in its artistic or metaphysical sense, is the realisation of an ideal, the likeness of thing to thought. Truth in these ways, is truth of word or of work, not truth of thought, for this is the likeness of thought to thing. Yet, mark how, in every kind, truth's needfulness is the condition and the measure of possible falsehood. Falsehood is not the mere absence of truth, but it is the want of truth when and where truth ought to be. Wherefore, thought is not false because it is deficient, but because it is wrong, not because it does not represent but because it misrepresents. That the mind can be mistaken is only possible in so far as it can fail to see the truth which it ought to recognise. The very energy and bent of mind towards truth renders it possible that it may slip into falsehood. Thought can only fail to truly image thing, because it is made to succeed. Therefore, that it does fail, is owing to its own imperfection, or to outward accident, or to adverse circumstance. But, again, imperfection supposes some power; accident cannot be either constant or necessary, and adverse circumstance may cease through change or be overcome by force. Hence, as it is in the nature of mind to represent reality, it must naturally tend to picture things truly, and, when its action is normal, its application befitting its power, and its surroundings suited to its kind, it must

succeed.   Sometimes, then, and in some things, mind
must be right.

It will be worth our while to dwell upon the reasonableness of our claim to true knowledge.   Here is another
way of getting a good look into the evidence of it.

Thought is an intellectual image, a mental expression,
an ideal reproduction of an object.   When this image is
like what it purports to represent, it is a true thought.
When it is unlike, it is false.   Falseness of thought is
not the mere absence of truth.   It is the absence of
truth that should be present.   Hence, a thought is not
false that is true as far as it goes, even though it stop
short, for this is only a limit to its likeness.   It is false
only where it begins to be positively unlike.   It is false
only in so far as it misrepresents.

Truth, in its logical sense, is the likeness of thought
to thing.   But, it is more than dead likeness, such as is
realised in the representation of a perfect portrait.   It
must be a living likeness.   It is the likeness of a living
principle.   Further, it must be more than a material
likeness of life, such as may be found between son and
father.   It must be a living likeness that is characteristic
of mind.   Now, the likeness that is characteristic of mind
is knowledge.

But knowledge is the living likeness of thought to
thing, which is recognised as a likeness that is true.
For a likeness that is unaware of its own truth is not
knowledge.   Thus knowledge includes, firstly, the intellectual image of a thing; secondly, the likeness of
this image to that thing; thirdly, the consciousness that
this thought is like that thing.   Wherefore, truth, in
its thorough sense, means true knowledge that is known
to be true.   For, indeed, when thought is said to be like

thing, it must be understood in a way that is true to the nature of thought. Now, this is none other than the conscious likeness of the knowing to the known.

At this point we may turn to examine a definite conclusion. I think $2 + 2 = 4$. It is most decidedly a fact that I think so. Again, it is also a fact that I can't help thinking so. I am aware of this. This fact is most clearly and unmistakably present to my mind. My thought correctly represents this fact. I know, then, that, in this case at least, thought is truly like thing, and knowledge really conformable to fact. Therefore I know this much, that my knowledge of my being unable to think otherwise is true. Therefore, I know that this knowledge is not false. But, I also know that it is not false because it is true, for this is merely a correlative aspect of the same certainty. Therefore, I know that it is not false by reason of its truth. But, this knowledge cannot exclude the possibility of its being false, by reason of its being true, unless it be in the very nature of truth to exclude falsehood. But, if it be in the very nature of truth to exclude falsehood, it follows that truth, in so far as it is true, excludes falsehood, in so far as this is the denial of it, just as fact, which is realised truth, in so far as it is fact, excludes nothingness, in so far as this is the absence of itself. But, this is the Principle of Contradiction applied to the logical and to the real order of things.

In this knowledge of which I speak, I am quite sure about the subjective necessity which constrains me to think as I do. I am also quite sure of the reality of the fact which I am constrained to admit, namely that I can't help thinking as I do. Again, I am quite sure about the truth of my knowledge of this fact. But, what is most important of all, I am quite sure that my knowledge does not create or invent the fact, but that the fact determines my knowledge by setting in motion those intellectual forces which compel me to recognise this fact as it really is.   Thus, in this case, my knowledge is a natural and necessary recognition of truth.   But, such intellectual action can only be explained by a natural bent of mind itself.   Wherefore in this case at least, it is from the nature of mind itself that comes the recognition of reality, its conformity to fact, its knowledge of truth.

But, if, in one case, true knowledge must be explained as a recognition of truth due to the nature of mind, then as the nature of mind cannot be other than itself, in no case can misrepresentation of truth come from the natural or the necessary bent of mind.   Therefore, whenever there is misrepresentation of truth it is unnatural and accidental.   It must come from the mischance of outward circumstance or from the mistake of inward weakness.   Thus, the mind may be at fault because of its being placed under unfair or unsuitable conditions. It may itself fail because of its powers being shortcoming. But, the recognition of truth is natural to it, and, within a certain sphere, however small this be, necessary to it as well.   It is, then, reasonable to admit our First Condition, that the mind can know truth.

Wherefore, that thought comes from an instinctive bent, or necessitating impulse, or natural mould, or individual kind of intellect, is no sufficient or ultimate explanation of knowledge.   All this, the very point at issue, is still to be explained.   Now, the only possible explanation of it, is, that mind is a representing faculty, naturally made to mirror fact, and that, therefore, thought, under natural and fit conditions, is a living expression of truth, an ideal reproduction of reality.

With regard to our knowledge of what is outside ourselves, we may at once set aside the very wild notion that God makes our thoughts, leaving us under the delusion that they are made by things. If God exists, He cannot betray us into useless and inevitable error. Nor need we waste words on the whimsical hypothesis, apparently borrowed from the Arabian Nights, that Genii of some kind or other are busy sticking thoughts into our heads. We have no serious choice except between the theory of thought creating thing, of mind merely fancying fact, and the theory of thing determining thought, of mind being, in some way, influenced by fact to represent it as it really is. The precise way in which this may happen is quite another question, into which we need not for the moment enter.

Yet, on the other hand, since many objects may crowd together in confusion; since the varying aspects of things may be both multitudinous and misleading; since many and different data may be required for a right judgment; since innumerable occasions may occur of letting slip some one or other necessary consideration; since countless obstacles may crop up to hinder the legitimate unfolding of argument; and since, above all, the power of our mind is weak, its steps unsteady, its vision short, its grasp unable to seize much, its memory unable to hold securely, its impatience precipitous; mind may often mistake phantom for fact, appearance for reality, falsehood for truth. But, surely, this is accident. It proves, indeed, that the mind is not infallible always and in all things. It does not prove that the mind is fallible always and in all things. It shows that while the mind may accidentally fail, it is yet made for truth, and that, under favourable conditions, it will find truth.

A mirror is made to reflect light and thus give a true image. It is not made to reflect darkness, for darkness cannot be reflected at all. Yet, a mirror may so far fail to reflect, as to give the appearance of darkness; or it may so distort what it reflects as to give an image that is false. Yet this false image is only possible because the mirror can, in some measure, reflect truly. It is not a false image that is, as it were, created. It is a truth that is faultfully portrayed. So under unfavourable circumstances or unfair conditions a mind may form a false conclusion. Therefore, in the full noontide of evidence, in the immediate presence of reality, when there is no difficulty from distance or darkness, no danger from shadow or screen, mind will recognise truth.

Here, then, we have our complete starting-point; the First Fact of our own existence; the First Principle of Contradiction; and the First Condition, that our mind can recognise truth. We have now a footing both in the physical order of reality, and in the logical order of thought, and we are able to join one with the other.

From the very fact of these being fountain-truths of evidence, we are powerless to prove them. Wherefore should any one still doubt about them, he must patiently seek, not for their proof, but for their reasonable explanation. Should any one deny them, we must fail to reach him. But, he is, thereby, himself, guilty of high-treason against common-sense. He is a rebel against reason. He is a logical outlaw.

CHAPTER III

POSSIBILITY

SECTION I. WHAT POSSIBILITY DOES NOT MEAN

THERE cannot be a real knowledge of nothing; for, nothing, being utter absence of truth, is not knowable. We cannot, then, think of what is not, except by representing it to our mind as though it were. Thus, we speak of falsehood as though it were a kind of truth. We speak of emptiness as if it were something solid. So, too, we talk and we think about unrealities as if in some sense they were real, and about mere possibilities as if they were in some way actual. These modes of thought are perfectly true and logical when they stop short at projecting their own shadows into the world outside them; when they do not make affirmations out of their own way of affirming; when, in other words, they do not transfer their own subjective manner of thinking into the objective matter of their thought. But, here, there is evident risk of unconsciously slipping into error. Thus, children take darkness to be something positive as light or air or cloud, and their fancy peoples it with ghosts. Itinerant tinkers speak about the holes in kettles and pans as though these were substantial framework to be clothed with solder and tin. Thus, again, men have written as though they believed nothing to be the happy mother of whatever is.

Possibility is not Actuality. It does not mean what is, but what can be. We do, indeed, think of it, as though, in some way, it were actual; but we do not affirm of it any existence neither an existence in the real order of things, nor even an existence in the logical order of thought except as a truth resulting from that real order. Possibility merely is and merely means the relation to fact which is included in the "can be" of what is not but may be fact.

Possibility and Actuality are correlative, not indeed as equal notions that are separable or as least distinct, but as the same notion in its ideal stage compared to its own realisation, as the thing that is a fact and the type of which it is the fulfilment. They explain each one the other. That is possible which may or can be actual. Possibility can only be explained by this relation. Actuality includes Possibility, and adds to it, not a mere relation, but a positive meaning in itself and a solid existence in fact. What is merely possible, considered exclusively in itself and of itself, is absolutely nothing, perfect vacancy, utter void, downright emptiness, pure simple unmitigated absence of anything. Possibility, then, does not mean Actuality.

SECTION 2. WHAT POSSIBILITY DOES MEAN

Possibility is the "can be" of Actuality. That is possible which may be actual. We have to develop the meaning of this. First of all, what is possible cannot be impossible. Now, that alone is impossible which includes within itself a contradiction. For as a contradiction in terms is a nonsense, so a contradiction in fact is a nonentity. The contradiction must of course, be real, not merely apparent. For instance, a man that is an irrational animal is a contradiction, and therefore an impossibility, if "irrational" be taken as denying the faculty of reason. But if "irrational" be taken to deny merely the use of reason, a man that is an irrational animal is not only a possibility, but a fact. We have lunatics inside our madhouses and outside them we meet with fools. The first condition, therefore, of Possibility is the absence of impossibility. This is the negative view. The ideas which are combined to make up the notion of anything must not clash together, so as to destroy one another. They must not involve such logical repugnance as would make their union a logical annihilation. Otherwise it would be possible for the fact of their union to prove the fact of its impossibility.

A positive aspect of Possibility is that the ideas combined are expressive of something and therefore positive. Thus, an irrational animal is possible. There is no repugnance in the existence of an Ass. Yet, this exclusion of reason positively determines the vague notion "animal" to a positive and particular kind. It is then, in reality, positive, though expressed in a negative form. Again, a pure negation is not possible. Therefore, mere absence of positive affinity and of positive contradiction is not possible. Therefore, when there is no positive contradiction between notions, there is a positive possibility of their being combined. Thus, Possibility means that the ideas combined to constitute the notion of a thing, express something positive and coalesce together so as to be not a mere straggling total of qualities but one consolidated unity in kind. This is the fuller meaning of Possibility. It is, however, all of it identically contained in the simple statement: Whatever is not impossible is possible.

This Possibility of which we have been speaking is intrinsic or internal to the thing possible. There is also external or extrinsic Possibility. It is the relation connoting the existence and power of a cause that can render actual what is merely possible, that can determine intrinsic Possibility to a real state of fact. Thus, a screech is intrinsically possible because there is no logical repugnance in that kind of inarticulate noise in the highest register of the human voice, with extreme loudness of tone and extreme harshness of vibration which frightened females or jocular tipplers sometimes emit. A screech is extrinsically possible, not simply of itself, but because of the people who can perpetrate it. Should there be no cause capable of producing it, a thing is not said to be extrinsically possible. But, we do not assume that there is any such cause. Whether things that are merely possible, require a cause to make them real; or whether they can create themselves; or whether they can drop from nowhere, for no reason and by no means, we shall see presently. What we want to see now is the meaning of that Possibility which is the intrinsic absence of self-contradiction.

SECTION 3.   THE REASON OF POSSIBILITY

Since what is merely possible has no actual existence, and is, therefore, simply and really nothing, it cannot have any actual or real reason for itself in itself. The reality of its logical existence in so far as this is a positive existence, depends altogether on the actuality of the thought which actually thinks of it. Thus, a man twenty feet tall is intrinsically possible, because there is no contradiction involved in the notion of such a being. But as a fact such a being does not exist, and consequently has no reality whatever of its own, therefore no reason that is real within itself. When we do think of so extensive a personage, he is present in our thought because he is the object of our meditation. In this way, he has a positive logical presence, the whole reality of which, however, comes all and comes only from the reality of our actual intellectual action. If no one ever thought of that particular possible gentleman, he never would have had even that positive logical reality which consists in being positively and really thought of. Would this have made him impossible? Certainly not. He is possible, whether we think of him or not. But would he still have had a real possibility? No positive reality; for, he would not have been, of course, a positive fact in existence, nor would he have had even the positive reality of logical supposition. Yet, for all that, as his actuality would involve no contradiction, he would still have been possible, in a purely negative sense, indeed, but still in a sense that is true. We might certainly say that he is really possible, by reference to a cause capable of creating him. But, it is plain that, in the first place, this sort of possibility is extrinsic; and secondly, that it supposes the object in question to be previously in itself possible. No object can be produced unless it is first possible. Its production does not make it possible. If actual production were alone needed to render a thing possible a square circle might be produced and so become possible. The reason why a square circle cannot be produced and a round one can, is that the first is impossible the second possible. Why is a round circle possible? Because there is no contradiction in it. Why is there no contradiction in it? Because it is the very nature, the inmost kind of a circle to be round. What is the reason of this? The absolute immutable eternal truth that a circle is and must be from always to always a circle. What is the reason of this? The logical necessity of a truth's identity with itself.

Have we got to the end yet? No. We have only got to this, that nothing is possible and nothing impossible, unless there be an absolute immutable and eternal necessity in truth. There is no reason why a circle should not be square, there is no possibility of a circle being round; unless a circle must absolutely be round. Hence, Possibility arises from a logical necessity which is absolute, changeless, and ceaseless. Here we are getting close to the point. What does this logical necessity come from? What is the reason of it? It is no fact that exists outside thought; yet, it is independent of thought; for, thought is determined by it; it is not determined by thought. There is, then, no reality in the absolute necessity of logical truth, that can give a real intrinsic self-sufficient reason for it. Wherefore, we must find the reason for it, where we find the reason for the whole logical order of things, in the real order of things. The real order of things which are not of themselves necessary or absolute, presupposes the logical order of things possible. This presupposes the absolute necessity of logical truth. But, again, the logical order presupposes the real, without which it is bald, bare, blank chaos. Truth is an intellectual echo, not a creation, of reality. Hence if there be any Possibility, it must be founded on an absolute necessity of logical truth. If there be any absolute necessity of logical truth, it must be founded on an absolute necessity of reality. Wherefore, that anything is or is not possible, has the final reason for the reality of its truth and for the truth of its reality, in an absolute, immutable, eternal, logical truth which is intrinsically real. In such a reality of necessity and necessity of reality, the logical and real orders of things must find an equal, identical, self-sufficient foundation in fact and an equal, identical, self-sufficient reality of reason.

CHAPTER IV

REALITY

SECTION I.   REALISED FACT

AMONGST sensible people, there is always to be found a good deal of honest veneration for facts. A fact is something concrete, tangible, obvious, practical. It is something done. There can be no doubt about its existence, and the certainty of its existence includes some share of certainty about its kind. A fact is the actuality of something possible. An impossibility cannot be a fact. A fact is something that has passed from the state of mere possibility into the state of actualised possibility. It has passed into the state of reality. Reality does not change the nature of what was possible. You yourself are exactly the same nature, whether you be considered as a mere possibility, or as a fact. You were possible with exactly the same length, breadth, and thickness which you at present enjoy. The amplitude or meagreness of your chin, the obtuse or acute angle of your nose, the colour of your eyes, and of your hair, the rotundity or the slimness of your frame, — all the details of your material conglomeration, — the inner qualities of your character, your selfishness, your conceitedness, your taste for unwholesome drinks, or for unbecoming fashions, your disinterested desire to devote your attention to other people's business, your serene reliance on the evidence of your own infallibility, your dauntless rejection of all wisdom offered by the wise, and of all example shown you by the holy, — these, with certain grains of common-sense and some few seeds of human kindliness, were the possible components which made up your possible self. You cannot possibly be any one else than your own self realised in fact. Thus the same identical nature may be either merely possible or it may be actual. The difference is not in the kind, but in the reality of the nature. The possible is the nature, as it is only logically true. The fact is that nature, as it is also actually existent. The possible is really nothing. The fact is really a fact. What is the reason of the reality of a fact? Some people say: "A fact is a fact, and that's all about it." This is generally a good and sufficient answer, when there is a question of eating one's dinner or of catching a train, or of curing a cold, or of snubbing the impertinence of inquisitive people. Some Positivists and Agnostics make use of it in Philosophy, where it is always utterly out of place, when they want to dodge a well-aimed argument or to discount a plain proof which they cannot barefacedly deny. It is not the sort of answer given by philosophers who use their common-sense to sift things thoroughly. If anything had always been a fact, there might be some apparent reason for asserting that this is reason enough to give for its reality. But, when we have a fact, which, however real it be now, was once merely possible, and therefore nothing real at all, then, there must be some reason for this coming of a fact out of nothing into reality. When we say that a fact comes out of nothing, we do not understand nothing to be a kind of canister, bottle, tub, or tin, in which possible facts are preserved ready for reality. We say that a fact comes from nothing in the sense, that, before it was a fact, it was not anything at all. Now that it is a fact, it has a reason for this reality, because there is nothing without a reason for it. We want to know the reason why a fact is a reality.

What a strange, morbid craving, men, successful in particular branches of science, seem to suffer from! They appear unable to restrain themselves from giving to the public, proofs of their ignorance and specimens of their dulness, not only in other studies outside their sphere, but even in the most elementary matters of common-sense. Again the affectation of ignorance and the insolence of cynicism are very contagious. Thus, on the one hand, foolish old scientists sometimes get muddled over the simplest problems of ordinary life; and, on the other hand, foolish young fops think it "the thing" to put on an air of dismal doubt about principles which they are never likely to get muddled over because they are never likely to get as deep into them as would bring them to the stage of muddle. Both these classes of men scoffingly deny or condescendingly doubt the Principle of Causality.

I once met an invalid lady, who bored all her visitors, with loud and long lamentations over her loss of appetite. She was able, indeed, sometimes to force herself to pick a few crumbs, or just barely taste a little beef-tea. She did not look starved. Her dearest and most trusted female friends, from the noblest motives, of course, eagerly seized on every possible opportunity to talk over the matter with everybody from a different point of view. The fact was that she absorbed quantities of nourishment, in both liquid and solid form, which would blunt the voracity of a school-boy, or strain the elasticity of an Alderman. This lady acted and spoke in the matter of food, as, in matters of Philosophy, act and speak our hippish Agnostics.

Speaking, not of the few who need pity and are silent, but of the many who want to be pitied and advertise their ills, a typical instance where the ridiculous and the pitiable phases of human life are met, is that of the fashionable Agnostic. His conversation, when he poses as the representative of Modern Thought, consists in great measure of woeful groanings over his imaginary doubts. Yet, the mass of adulterated facts which he greedily admits, if only they be labelled "Science," and the multitude of mixed-up principles which he blindly adopts, when they are recommended by "The Age" is simply astounding.

When one of these noble scions of Modern Thought becomes conscious that he is expected to vouchsafe to the Universe some words of wisdom, — whether it be in an interval between the circling inspirations of Champagne, or from amidst the fragrant halo of a cigarette, or when enthroned and worshipped with all the bewildering blandishments of a drawing-room, — he clears the aeolian raptures of his throat with a passing wave of music, half thrilling sigh, half soul-subduing sob; lifts the rose-tipped tenderness of his finger, to soothe the coquettish waywardness of his moustache, arches the shadowed stateliness of his brow into rippling ridges of solemn meditation, like moon-lit waters fraught with mysterious messages from far-off spheres, fixes his intuitive gaze upon the furthest and faintest horizon of the "Knowable" with the lofty melancholy of a soul that speaks in inconsolable sadness, yet suffers in pathetic heroism; and, falteringly, murmurs, "To my mind there appears no reason for supposing the necessity of a cause." All such suppositions have given way before the "Exact Science" of the "Age." — *Causa finita est.* Let Aristotle think no more. Let Plato sleep, and Socrates be dumb. Let the great intellects of old times be told that, because they did not travel in trains nor read newspapers, they were unfit to follow a Syllogism or to grasp a proof in Euclid. Let Philosophers be ignored that are not of the "Age." The world must begin anew. For the first time, Wisdom has dawned upon the earth. A young gentleman who has been reading the prose-poetry of a learned lecturer had delivered himself of a doubt. Think no more. *Causa finita est.*

Then the hero descends from his mental pedestal, and, with a keen practical appreciation of the real relation between cause and effect, sips his glass of dainty wine, or takes a cup of comfortable tea. But, on the conscious paint of girl-like lips there quiver, in modulated undulations of mingled gratitude and regret, the words, "Exact Science;" while from the hollow hearts and jaded wits of Dame Philosophers, or blue-stocking Demagogues, through distant vistas of fruitless flirting, from out the monotonous records of years lost in waiting, there is whispered a melancholy echo, "Age." Then the curtain falls, and, until the next *coup de théâtre*, all retire home to their common-sense.

What on earth is this terrible "Principle of Causality," which not only flutters "the dove-cots where spinsterhood sours into strongmindedness," but which stirs up all the spite and spleen of one immoral Atheist, and goads into froth and fury every inch of another arrogant Agnostic? Nothing more nor less than what every man, woman, and child, Atheist and Agnostic included, was, is, and ever will be thoroughly persuaded of; nothing more nor less than that whatever has not within itself the full and final reason for its reality, must have, if real, a real reason for its reality, outside itself. Therefore, it means, first of all, that nothing is nothing. It means, besides, that nothing cannot do or make anything. Then, it means that nothing cannot make itself into something. It means that for whatever is real, there is a positive and real reason, not a simple negation or mere absence of reason. It means that whatever is now real, and was not real, did not get its reality from its own nothingness, nor from any other nothingness. It means that whatever really begins to be real has a real reason for its reality, outside itself, that is to say, a real cause.

To deny this principle is to deny without reason what all reasonable people admit; for, there can be no difficulty in seeing that common-sense is on our side on this point at least, that there can be no reason given for not having a real reason for a real reality. To doubt this principle is to allow one's ignorance of theoretic and scientific proof to set aside one's practical knowledge of fact. We would scarcely consider it a proof of cleverness, if a man were to deny or doubt the existence of railways, because he did not thoroughly understand the mechanism of a locomotive. Neither does it show extreme talent to deny or doubt that a fact is an effect because one has not mastered the metaphysics of action. It cannot be held that the absence of reason is an evidence of truth. Neither can the absence of reality be an explanation of fact. Now, to refuse all explanation as to why a fact is a fact, is to run away out of the lists. To offer the fact which was not a fact, as sufficient explanation of why it is a fact, is either to draw its proof from its supposition or to derive its reality from its unreality.

A realised fact is the actuality of what was intrinsically possible, which results from the real action of a real cause, in relation to which that fact was extrinsically possible. A realised fact is a realised effect, a reality which is real result, and therefore real proof of a real cause.

SECTION 2.   REALISED TRUTH

Il n'y a rien d'insolent comme un fait. A fact has a most uncompromising and outrageous way of giving the lie to troublesome theorists. It is a realised truth. Men who write pretty phrases about "Our Father-Man," or about "Infinite horizons" and "melting into evening air," or about "Idealism," or about "the greatest sum of happiness of the greatest number," appear to entertain a violent antipathy to anyone else who writes about abstract truth. Let them have their own whim for the moment. We need not take the button off our rapier for them. Leaving aside facts that are only reached by intellect, take such facts as might come under the observation of a cow. See what they have got to teach us. There is no denying a fact. Take your first fact, your own existence. What an immensity of truth you find involved therein! Every truth included in your possibility is realised in your actuality. If it be true that you are, this fact is the realisation, in concrete existence, of every abstract truth bound up with your living being. Hence, you are a living verification of certain principles of Chemistry, of Botany, and of Zoology. You are a tangible proof of the possibility of mind and matter forming one true substance. You are the law of Gravitation in practical working order. The theories of Optics are facts in your eyes. The number of truths which actually exist within you, not in mere poetic imagination, nor in scientific castles-in-the-air; not in the day-dreams of reviewers, nor in the phantasies of professors; not in the idealisation of lecturers, nor in the contemplation of philosophers; but in downright, thorough, solid, humdrum fact, is almost endless. Understand well the simple accuracy of this. Each and every fact is a truth. It is not a mere abstract truth; but it is a truth, which, while it may be reflected in mind under one aspect alone, and therefore in an abstract manner, is yet itself, in very deed, concrete and existent. It is not only true, but it is also real. It is a realised truth. It is a fact.

Now, the truth realised in a fact, is, in a logical sense, more necessary and forceful as to the more general and abstract notions which it involves, than it is as to the more detailed and narrower notions which it verifies. As a truth is more universal, so is it more fundamental in logic, and more absolute in evidence. Thus, if the least, the lowest, and the last truth which is realised in your person, be true, much more must those truths be really true which this last truth presupposes for the possibility of its truth. Thus, if you are a man, you must, with greater reason be admitted to be an animal. For you cannot possibly be a man unless it be first true, in logical sequence, that you are an animal. It is quite possible that a fact should have the realised truth of an animal in it; and yet not have that additional truth in it which would be required to bring it to the further reality of the truth that is realised in man.

A fact is an argument that is not easily got rid of. There is a great deal of truth in it, and every tittle of that truth is real. You and I can take its truth to pieces in our thought; but all these abstractions have one and the same foundation for their multitudinous intellectual images, in the one true nature of the fact in which all of them undividedly are realised.

SECTION 3. REALISED CONDITIONS

Not only does a fact hold within itself the actual reality of many truths; it also affirms and proves those conditions to have been realised without which it could not be real. The fact of the realised truth of an egg proves, physically speaking, the existence in fact of a real hen. Eggs do not grow out of nothing. Again, some geologists are very anxious to have us believe that coal is a result of formative forces working, during prodigiously protracted periods, upon vegetable matter. They can't give us coal unless there was vegetable matter for the making of it. But, the reality of vegetable matter, as it was being turned into coal, was a real consequence of the reality of trees. Wherefore, the former reality of trees is a condition realised in the actual reality of the coal.

When a consequence requires for its reality the actual existence of a real condition, that condition's truth is realised, as in a real proof, in the reality of that consequence. Thus, the actual existence of oxygen in the air, is a condition realised in the reality of your life. What cannot be real without the real existence of something else is a real proof, in cold, hard, stern fact, when it is itself a fact, that the something else in question is real.   It is a real consequence of a real condition.

CHAPTER V

*THE FIRST REALITY OF FACTS, AND THE FINAL
TRUTH OF REASONS*

SECTION I. FACTS THAT ARE NOT FIRST AND REASONS THAT ARE NOT FINAL

WHEN speaking of the starting-point of Philosophy,
we found that it includes the First Fact, in the order
of recognised reality, the First Principle, in the order of
evident truth, and the First Condition, in the order of
mental certainty. It is plain that such a starting-point
is subjective. It is the starting-point of thought, not
of thing. It is the beginning of our knowledge, not of
nature. It is the foundation of Science, not of the
Universe. As the mind is to advance in knowledge, it
must begin from what is nearest to itself. Its progress
is towards the perfection of knowledge, and this is
reached when the mind has got to those evident and
ultimate reasons for things, which are the clear and
absolute answer of what in reality is first and most
fundamental. Setting forth from our starting-point,
we want now, to look for what is first, not in our knowledge, but in the knowable; not in our own mental
mirror, but in the world and wisdom that are outside
ourselves.

From a want of right balance at the start, even great
philosophers have stumbled straight away, and their

systems have been, in consequence, maimed and crippled throughout. Thus, for instance, the Scotch School, being unable to prove the First Condition, and being unwilling to admit it on reasonable explanation, has sought to change the definition of certainty from a natural recognition of objective truth into a blind yielding to subjective force; so that, as far as philosophers can, they destroy the reality of knowledge, and the value of evidence. The Positivists, from an exclusive attention to Fact, which, though from different reasons, stirs the sympathies of the French as well as of the English mind, slide into a denial of all abstract principle and of all intellectual conditions, until they come to confound the logical order of thought with the action and reaction of mere material force. The German mind, on the other hand, became exclusive in its abstract reasonings. Hence, when the great intellect of Kant, leaving Fact out of Focus, turned all its power towards making Thought the explanation, as well as the recognition of all truth, he, naturally enough, admitted that mental judgments may be creative, as well as reflective of truth. His followers pushed his system further on. First, they reached the point where their system of reasoning fused the whole order of Fact into a mere abstract progression of Logic. Then they turned their method of examination against the First Principle, until they found the apex of their philosophy in the identity of Contradictories.

To found one's Philosophy exclusively on Fact, leads to Materialism. To found it exclusively on Truth, leads to Idealism. To found it exclusively on Thought, leads to Scepticism. But, excess always brings a reaction. Philosophies that are too exclusive, through unwarrantable negation or neglect, become, in their working out, too fanciful in affirmation, and too creative of Conclusions where their premises stop short.

Now, taking our stand at the starting-point which we have already examined, and which, it would seem, we have found to be fairly solid, full, and secure, we will look out over the universe. We get to know many facts which certainly are not first. We ourselves are not first facts. We are the results of other realities. We are the effects of other causes. But, nothing that is result or effect is a first fact. Hence, whatever owes its origin to a fact that precedes it, is a derived reality.

Further, whatever owes its reality, or any mode or manner of its reality, to the actual influence of another fact, is a dependent reality, a secondary fact. It may not be of an inferior kind; it may be simply superior in sort to that which acts upon it; but, whatever is acted upon, in so far as it is acted upon, and in that phase of real result which is realised within it by such real action, is a derived reality. Now, a derived reality, however little reality it owes to another fact, is not a first fact. A first fact must be understood to be a fact that is, in no way, derived; for, if it be, in any way, derived, it is, in some way, result or effect, and so it is not simply first. A first fact must have, of itself and by itself, its own full and thorough realisation. A fact that falls short of this, is not self-sufficing in its own reality, nor is it the adequate explanation of itself. A fact is either absolutely independent of all other fact for its own reality, or it is a derived reality. Self-evolution from possessed power to outward or inward act, is possible. Self-evolution from possibility to reality is not possible. What is nothing, and in so far as it is nothing, cannot make itself into something. What is merely possible, in so far as it is merely possible, is really nothing. It cannot, then, render itself actual. Unreality cannot realise itself. This is true, not only in the production of complete and substantial effects, not only in the making of direct and entire results, but also in every mode and modification by which any sort of reality that was previously merely possible, becomes a fact. Wherefore, there are many facts which are not first. Whatever has been realised in fact, whether completely or in part, by the agency of another reality, is only itself a dependent, secondary, derived reality. It is not a first fact. Therefore, philosophers must pass beyond and behind it, to look for the real reason in fact, and for the actual explanation in existence, of its reality.

In the same way, truths that depend on other truths are not supreme principles, and do not therefore give reasons that are final. The very notion of Science involves the idea of an organised body of principles, some of which are simple, universal, abstract, others more and more complex, more and more concrete, less and less wide, until individual conclusions are reached. The proof of a conclusion is in the reason got from a principle. This principle is proved by the reason got from a principle higher than itself. Thus, the final reason given by any science is the setting forth of its own first principles. No science can prove its own first principles. But, as there is harmony among principles, so is there also order among sciences. The first principles of each lesser science are proved by a higher science. In the end we come to the first Science, Philosophy, the first principles of which are the starting-point of knowl-

edge.   Now, speaking, not of the order in our knowing
of reasons, but of the order among the reasons themselves which are knowable, we see clearly that there
are many reasons, which are not final, many which need
further argument for their proof, and, for their explanation, other evidence.

We want to get above all facts that are effects, and
beyond all truths that are conclusions.   Is there a First
Fact to which all reality owes its origin?   Is there a
Final Reason from which each and every other truth
borrows light?

SECTION 2.   CAN THE UNIVERSE EXIST AS A MUTUAL
AID SOCIETY?

Can facts that are not first stand alone?   Can realities that are derived club together so as to furnish a
joint-stock existence, which, although it is owned only
dependently and in part by each, may yet be an independent and final reason for the universe of them all?
We have to think this out.   We begin by disentangling
different threads of combination, which may or may
not enable units to work into one collective result.

If a very heavy load is to be carried from one place
in the country to another, when the weather is wet and
the roads bad, it is likely enough that one cart-horse
will not be able for the work.   Even should two horses
fail to stir the waggon, others can be yoked, until in the
end the huge mass creaks, jolts, splashes, and crashes
along.   If one horse cannot draw a cart, many can.
The greater the horse-power you can command, the
greater the weight you can move.

If you have a pretty string of pearls in a necklace or

a rich ruby in a ring, you will yet find it hard to get one or the other to talk to you. You may put both together; you may call on the help of unsophisticated stones, smashed by stupid labourers to be strewn over simple streets; you may concentrate the strength and splendour of diamonds, that flash over the brows of queens; you may gather the multitudes of the pebbles that sparkle in the fringe of the sea; you may combine the chiselled blocks of the Pyramids with the untamed massiveness of mountain rocks; yet, in the end, you will be just as powerless to coax or force one simple word out of them all. Is not this very simple? Yes; so dreadfully simple as to be beneath the notice of "Modern Thought."

Some modern philosophers condescendingly assure us that we can never reason from an individual to a collection. Others serenely regret that we cannot conclude anything at all from the nature of a thing. But, really, although from the individual fact that John Stuart Mill proves by a Syllogism that a syllogism does not prove, I cannot argue that all men's logic is illogical, yet, from the fact, that John Stuart Mill was "mortal," I can infer that all men are and must naturally be "mortal." From the fact that one horse cannot draw a load, I cannot conclude that four horses cannot draw it. From the fact that one stone cannot talk, I can conclude that no number of stones can talk. Why? What rational rule are we to follow in such reasonings? This.

What is true of one individual thing on account of its own distinct and particular self, on account of its own individuality, cannot, for this reason alone, be taken to be true of another. But, what is true of it on account of its nature, is, therefore, true of every other individual of the same nature. Thus you may be a snob on your own account: you are an animal on account of your kind. Hence, I can gather that every other man is an animal. Not that every other man is a snob. Look to the grounds for this statement. What can be truly said of anything, must have some definite reason for its truth. This reason it is that limits or extends the application of what is said.

Distinct reasons for a conclusion may be drawn from the same reality. Thus, the same man may be my friend, because he is a relation, because he is kindhearted, because he rides well to hounds, because he plays a good game of whist, and because he owes me money. On the other hand, there may be reasons why I do not accept his invitation to spend a week with him at Christmas. But each one of these reasons is founded either upon the individual and personal character of the man, or upon qualities common to others. If my reason be taken from what is individual, my conclusion can go no further than the gentleman in question. Should my reason come from that nature which makes him akin to all, my conclusion will suit the others too.

Hence, because speech is absolutely excluded by the nature of a stone, I must deny the possibility of speech to any stone. Because the faculty of reason is an attribute of human nature, I must in virtue of this knowledge say that each man has the faculty, even though he may not have the use, of reason.

Again, a collection may give a reason for an assertion about itself. Thus, twelve horses make a dozen, and, twelve horses can pull a load which one horse cannot pull. Note, however, that between these two reasons for statements, there is a difference. The dozen arises directly from the collection itself. The pulling power arises from the individual horses that make up the dozen.

Having thus laid down our broad lines of thought, we go on to affirm, in the first place, that a number of individuals can combine to justify a collective conclusion, either when the reason for this is partially realised in each, or when such reason is furnished by the collection itself. Twelve horses can pull a load, because each horse can pull a certain portion of it. Twelve horses make a dozen, because the collection and the dozen are identical. In the second place, when the reason for or against a conclusion is absolutely involved, not in the mere individuality, but in the very nature of a thing, no multiplication can change that conclusion. The proof is plain. Multiplication only adds. It cannot change. No multiplication of saddles will give you a horse.

Now come to the application of these principles. In virtue of what reason, does existence belong to the things which make up our Universe? Does each exist by reason of its own individuality? No; because each may cease to be existing, but nothing can cease to be itself. Does each exist by reason of its nature? No; because, in that case, all individuals of the same nature would, for the same reason, always and of necessity, exist. Does the collective universe exist of itself? No; because the collective universe is nothing more than the things that compose it. But, such collection is not identical with self-existence in the way in which a dozen is identical with twelve. For, no contradiction is involved in the hypothesis of its non-existence. Neither is the universe self-existent by the combination of partial powers in the individuals. For, in the first place, the sum total cannot be necessary when any multitude of the subscribers may fail, and when no number or kind of them is necessarily given. The resultant pull of twelve horses cannot be a necessary fact, when none of the horses are of necessity forthcoming. Besides, self-existence is not partially produced by the units of the collection. For each one of them, as far as its own self and nature go, is absolutely and utterly without any reason for actual existence. Each of them exists by reason of an actual realisation not determined by itself. Of themselves, they are all in the region of mere abstract logic, — thinkable as possible, nothing in fact. Of themselves, they are altogether and absolutely without reality to determine, without reason to explain, this infinite transit from the region of what is possible, to the world of actual fact.

Weigh these matters well. The existence of all things in the world is contingent, that is to say, they happen to be or not to be. Rather, it happens to them that they are existent, or are not existent. As far as their own nature merely is concerned, we have no reason for asserting that they do exist. Nay, if we have no more reason for actual existence than is contained in their own nature, we must assert that they do not exist. The possibility of existence is, indeed, involved in the very notion of their nature. For, a nature which is not possible to exist, is impossible, and therefore an absurdity, and therefore no nature at all. On the other hand, actual existence is quite outside the notion of anything contingent. When a contingent nature does actually exist, it is a fact. But, this very fact is exactly what we have got to find a reason for. It is not an actual fact by reason of its own nature. What belongs to it by reason of its own nature, is absolutely necessary to the very notion of it, whereas its actual existence is quite contingent. You are unthinkable except as a human being, but this does not at all imply that you are an actual fact. Living or dead, you are a man. If you are alive, it happens to yourself to be existing. If you are dead, it happens to your same self not to exist. Were the actual existence to have its reason in your nature, it would be as absurd to say that you could ever cease to exist, as to say that you are a man who is not a man. Again, were a being to exist so as to be a fact, by reason of its own special self, rather than by reason of its general kind, it would be self-existent by reason of its own individuality. But, a being such as this could admit no more change, or limit in its existence, than it could admit limit or change in its own identity. Neither could any outside action interfere with its existence. For no outside action can make one identity into another. In one word, contingent and self-existent are contradictory.

We have, then, this point; a contingent being is not the reason of its own existence. Now, in what way is this true? Is it true only in the way in which one horse is unable to draw a huge load, or in the way in which one stone is unable to make a brilliant speech? I answer: All contingent things fall as far short of being a real reason for actual existence as all stones fall short of being a real source of oratory.

Mark the exact point of comparison. It is this: From the truth that it is utterly foreign to the nature of a stone to speak, I conclude that no infinity or variety of stones can speak; for, number does not change nature.

So, from the fact that it is utterly contrary to the nature of contingent being to give a sufficient reason for actual existence, I conclude that no multitude or diversity of contingent beings can give a sufficient reason for actual existence.

You may unconsciously try to shift the question. You may say: surely, one tree is quite sufficient reason, with average soil, sun, and shower, to account for the actual existence of another tree that grows from its seed. I answer. It is quite outside the question, whether one actual tree can produce another actual tree, or not. You really assume what is in question, namely, actual existence. Your first tree, your earth, your sun, your everything contingent is, of itself, absolutely non-existent. How do these things happen to be? See our point. We are not speaking of mere chronological succession. Were this the question, you might run away from behind one actual tree to a previous one and so on back for ever. This would, indeed, force you to assume that by making the difficulty infinite, you could get rid of it. But postulating an infinite number of bricks, could you get them to support one another upon a basis of nothing? Given an endless series of hot-water pipes, can you do without a bunker? Is an infinite string of conclusions to be proved without a principle, or an infinite result of actual existence to be explained by an infinite absence of it? That, however, we need not develop. What we are talking about is not chronological succession, but logical sequence. A conclusion actually implies a principle. The hypothetical actually supposes the absolute. The contingent actually rests upon the necessary.

Now, take in thought the whole universe as it is made

up of things that may or may not exist. Let us not quarrel about words. Do you admit that there is anything simply absolute, necessary, self-existent? If you do, you admit all that I want. If you once admit this much, you admit God, whether you are quite aware of it or not. If you do not admit the logical necessity of something existing of itself, so that in its very nature is involved the notion of actual and absolutely self-owned existence, then, you admit that all things are contingent. But, if all things are contingent, there is nothing real. For, if all things are contingent, there is nothing except what of itself does not exist. Therefore, there is nothing except what of itself is only possible to exist. But, what of itself is only possible to exist, is of itself really nothing. Therefore, all things are, of themselves, really nothing. Therefore, it is impossible that anything should be real.

More than this. Speech is impossible to a stone. Therefore, no infinite collection of stones can speak. Self-existence is impossible to a contingent being. Therefore, no infinite collection of contingent beings can be self-existent. But, if there be nothing self-existent, all things are non-existent. They have no existence of themselves, nor is there another from which to get it. Therefore, again, if all things are contingent, there is nothing real.

Wherefore, the Universe of contingent things cannot be, in the matter of existence at least, a mere Mutual Aid Society. In the first place, it cannot possibly be self-existent. In the second place, it cannot exist at all, unless there be something self-existent from which alone can be got the reality or the reason of it.

SECTION 3. A FIRST FACT THAT IS FINAL TRUTH

We cannot reasonably expect to have fresh eggs unless there be hens to lay them. These hens cannot naturally have come to light except through an opening in an egg-shell. Some philosophers get very much addled over these eggs. They cannot make up their minds whether to begin with an egg, or with a hen. If ever there was a beginning at all, however fabulously distant that period may be, one or the other must have been first. Let us suppose that the series began with the hen. That hen must also have had a beginning. You can scarcely hope to start your series with an eternal hen. But, if even that hen had a beginning there was a moment before she began to be, when the whole series was merely possible, that is to say: really nothing. This reasoning is applicable to all things that had a beginning; thence if there was ever a moment when the Universe began to exist, there was a previous moment when there was nothing. Now, in that previous moment, either there was a First Fact always and for ever existing, by reason of its own absolute and independent necessity, or we are driven to assume, that, in the utter and sheer absence of anything, there can, without reason and without reality, bloom forth out of nothingness, a truth that is a conclusion without a principle to justify it; a fact that is a result without a power to determine it. This latter alternative is too much even for the omnivorous credulity of "Original Thinkers." It is in direct contradiction to every judgment of thought, and to every experience of life.

What is true in the hypothesis of a beginning in time,

is equally true in the other hypothesis, namely, that there has been no beginning in time. We cannot get rid of the logical necessity of derived truths depending upon self-evident principles, nor of the physical necessity of contingent realities depending upon self-owned existence.

As thought cannot conceive science to have been evolved out of mere blank emptiness of truth, so neither can it imagine reality that has developed itself out of void. Not even the sweetest prose-poetry of the self-sent prophets of the "Age" can disguise the dose concentrated in the supposition that nothing can account for something.

As we said above, if all things are contingent, there is nothing real. If all things are of themselves merely possible, there is nothing actual. There is, in the entire expanse of thought or thing, no foundation for truth, nor any reason for reality, unless, in logical and actual priority to what is hypothetical, relative, dependent, contingent, possible, there exist something absolutely true and eternally real.

Come back for a moment to the steam-engine. If you want the wheels to go round, you must get up steam. If, instead of getting up steam, you add another set of wheels, they are not one bit more likely to move. If, in order to explain why the wheels of a particular commonplace locomotive do as a matter of fact revolve, you postulate an infinite series of wheels, each set of which is worked by the one preceding, you are not talking like an engine-driver nor like an engineer, but like an Agnostic. If, in order to account for the same phenomenon you assert that the movement of the wheels requires neither steam nor any other motive power, whatever, but is simply evolved out of the infinite potentialities of the "Unknowable," then, my dear fellow, you are not talking like a mathematician, nor like a philosopher, nor like a sharp street Arab, nor like an honest country lout, you are only talking like a fashionable lecturer on "Exact Science."

Again, look at this question in the light of what has been said about Realised Facts, Realised Truths, and Realised Conditions. The reality of contingent things is the reality of a consequence, which is a proof, in fact, that the conditions on which it essentially depends are also real. Therefore, a necessary reality, without which there is nothing real, is affirmed, by the reality of the universe, to be a fact.

If there be no necessary truth, all propositions may indifferently be either true or false; or rather, no proposition is either true or false. If there be no necessary reality, all reality is without reality, that is to say, there is nothing real. All reason and all reality suppose an absolute necessity which is of itself both true and real. As nothing is real that is not possible, so nothing is possible unless there be an absolute necessity which makes it true, an absolute fact which can render it real.

A necessary reality, a reality that exists simply and absolutely of itself, is a First Fact; because, whether there be a question of a beginning in time or of a dependence in actuality, it is an ample and ultimate foundation for the universe of realities which do not of themselves exist. It is also a Final Reason; because it is a full explanation of the actual existence of things beyond the bare possibility of them; and because, without such explanation, logic is adrift from fact.

CHAPTER VI

IS THERE A GOD?

SECTION I.   ATHEISTS AND AGNOSTICS

MOST men who are convinced of the existence of God are unable to understand how anyone can really doubt about it.   They have a very wholesome disinclination to accept as thoroughly solid or thoroughly sincere those drastic statements which sweep aside all religion and which shift morality from its foundations upon Right to a basis of Pleasure.   They simply cannot admit Atheists to be anything but sophists or eccentricities.

Yet, men who read much ephemeral literature must wonder at the quantity of dust raised by reviews over this matter, and they must feel a sort of mental uneasiness at the growth in intensity and in volume of outcries against God.   Those who not only read but think, look for an explanation of this phenomenon.

Now, it were foolish as well as unfair to class all Atheists together.   Whatever may be said of the rest, some of them are truthful and intelligent, honourable and well-living.   As far as we can know anything, we know that some of those who call themselves Atheists or Agnostics are not only clever but also sincere.   It is a fact and we have got to account for it.   How is it that unbelief is not only very fashionable among the silly who chatter and the bad who bluster, but is to be met with amongst good men who use their wits and hold their tongue?

There is much waste of eloquence and argument, if they are not delivered with accurate aim. Two kinds of Atheism, which are quite apart from each other, are often supposed to hold the same position. Positive or Dogmatic Atheism asserts that God does not exist. It positively maintains that there is no God. Negative Atheism or Agnosticism neither denies nor affirms the existence of God. It maintains at most that the existence of God cannot be proved, or at least that the existence of God has not been proved. The Positive Atheist denies the reality of God as a fact. The Negative Atheist denies the evidence of God as a proof. The Positive Atheist declares that God is a mere myth of poetry or a monstrosity of superstition, and this he must undertake to show. The Negative Atheist stops short at saying that whether God do really exist or no, there is no sufficient warrant for our saying that God does exist.

First, we will take Positive Atheism. It is not merely unconvinced of God's existence; but it is convinced that there is no such thing as God. Mark, here, that this position could not be justified by any failure to prove God's existence. Such failure may, if it occur, justify Negative Atheism; but it is illogical to pass straightway from the absence of evidence to the denial of reality.

Now, bluntly and emphatically, in every Positive Atheist there is either a mental or a moral flaw. The mental flaw is in taking the idea of God to represent so gross and so grotesque an absurdity, that it requires great broadmindedness to suppose them not to be consciously dishonest. Then, they set about proving this notion, which no one ever had of God, to be unreal. Or, again, because something is said about the nature of God, whether rightly or wrongly does not matter, which they think to be unreasonable, they at once deny, not only the kind, but the fact of God. Just as if one were to deny that there had been any influenza because doctors differ as to the nature of it.

But, indeed, Positive Atheism, as a rational conviction, is impossible. It is absolutely impossible that any direct positive proof whatsoever should be brought against the existence of God.

We undertake to show that there cannot be any reason in a positive denial of God's existence. Were there any such reason, it must be either immediately evident to the mind, or reached through the medium of proof. The first supposition is simply absurd. Were it verified, all men would know that God does not exist, as plainly and undeniably, as each man knows that he himself does exist.

Nor can the other supposition stand, namely, that the non-existence of God can be drawn as a conclusion from another truth that is evident. Here, again, we have to treat separately two possible kinds of conclusion. When a truth is not self-evident, the reason of it must be got from the evidence of another truth, between which and itself there is a necessary logical sequence. Now, this necessary logical sequence is either from above or from below. The proving truth is either prior, as a principle, in the order of logical necessity, as well as in the order in which we gather our knowledge, to the proven truth, or the proving truth is only a consequence in the objective order of logic, of the truth which is proved, although, as it cannot be true unless the other be true, it leads us back to the knowledge of its necessary principle. The reasoning in an argument is either a following down from principle or cause to necessary consequence or effect; or it is a following up from consequence or effect to a necessary principle or cause.

Now, the very first and simplest notion of God excludes the possibility of any higher principle or cause. To suppose any principle or cause prior to God, is to suppose that God is not God. The only way in which an attempt of this kind might be made is by starting from abstract principles which in our mind are prior to our knowledge of God, and, by their means, seeking to fix upon some contradiction in the notion of a God. But such an attempt must plainly fail unless the notion of God be plainly falsified. The notion of God as existing includes no more than the notion of existence and the notion of necessity. But, neither in one or the other of these notions, nor in their combination is there any possible contradiction. Any further or fuller notion of God is a notion which involves, above what is needed for the existence of a God, something more about the nature of the God who exists. These notions are the subject matter, not of Theism, but of Theology. The notion of God which, if it be shown to be true, is sufficient to overthrow Atheism, is absolutely free from intrinsic contradiction.

Neither can the existence of God be disproved by that line of reasoning which from effect or consequence runs up back to cause or principle. In those material studies which, in the minds of some men, monopolise the name of science, we are accustomed from results known through experience or experiment to prove the presence or the kind of things. If this process or argument be not a secure road to truth, there is no reality in natural science. Can it be shown in this way that there is no God? No. Firstly: a result, an effect, or a consequence can prove the existence of a reality, of a cause, or of a principle. Even an Agnostic would scarcely say that an effect positively disproves the existence of a cause. Secondly: either we can logically infer from the existence of the world that there exists a First Cause or we cannot infer this. If we can, it follows that an Atheist is a Sophist. If we cannot, we must only say that we cannot either prove or disprove the existence of God; for, if we do not admit the world to be an effect, we lose all ground for any reasoning from the fact of its existence, either in favour of the existence of a God or against it. Some Atheists admit the principle of Causality when it seems to be on their own side, but not when it is against them. Even were we unable to prove the existence of a God, a Positive Atheist would have no excuse for changing his ignorance and doubt into dogmatism and denial. Thirdly: if actual facts ever afford a reasonable basis from which one may logically reach to the existence and kind of other facts, we can go on to say that, as the world is a fact, it not only does not disprove the existence of any fact which it supposes, but positively proves it. Therefore, just as, whatever difficulty we may have in understanding facts, or however contradictory they may appear to be, once we know them to be facts, we cannot deny their existence; so, once we know facts to be effects, we cannot deny the existence of their cause, no matter how impossible it may be to diagnose the nature of it. We may remain helplessly in a very fog of doubt as to the kind of the cause in question, but no matter how dark and impenetrable the gloom which hangs over this point, we can never conclude that this cause does not exist. You would not deny the reality of magnetism, even though, amongst all the theories put forth to explain its nature, no one should appear to you to be tenable. Now, if facts have any cause, it is impossible to deny the existence of a First Cause. The reason for admitting any Cause, is that these facts are not their own adequate explanation in logic or in reality. Therefore, facts must have some adequate explanation in reality and in logic. This is a First Cause. Again; if facts have any Cause, none of those facts which, to men, morbidly striving after "Original Thought," appear to be monstrosities, disprove their Cause, whatever it be. But, whatever this Cause be, it must meet the same questions as a First Cause, and yet it must fail to give a full and final answer unless it be a First Cause. If, on the other hand, facts have no cause, men have no science. For what Causality is in the order of fact, consequence is in the order of logic. They are two phases of the same principle. If facts have no cause, realities have no connection, reasons have no sequence, proofs have no power.

Thus, in very truth, the denial of Causality is a denial of knowledge. Doubt about causality is paralysis of Certainty. Further; any argument brought against a First Cause must either attempt to disprove the existence of any cause whatever, or it must meddle with the ulterior nature, beyond the mere existence of a First Cause; for, that it is First, presents no new difficulty until we come to questions about thought and will and personality. But, these are altogether outside the question of Existence. See, then, if you try to prove that there cannot be any cause, you are leaning upon the very principle which you deny, namely, that there is a real, and therefore a logical connection between a result and that from which it comes. If you try to disprove the existence of a First Cause, by arguments against its nature, you ought logically to maintain that there are no poems of Homer and no plays of Shakespeare, because you do not know all about the life and character of the author. Those poems and plays are facts. They were written by somebody. The name of the number, the country or the character of the author or authors, is outside the question. The poems and plays had an author. The world is a fact. It has an author. We have as yet nothing to do with questions of kind. We merely state the bald fact. The world has a Cause. Positive Atheists deny this. But, even had they reason for doubt, they can have no reason for this denial.

Wherefore, from first to last, a Positive Atheist either ventures, without any reason whatever, upon a dogmatic denial of what has always appeared evident to the vast majority of men; or he offers as proof the very reason which he himself denies; or he incurs the censure of all wise men, because, in the words of Aristotle, "It is a fool's part to give up a truth on account of the difficulties that arise out of it."

So far, we have spoken of the mental flaw in Positive Atheism. It is impossible to avoid speaking of the more common cause of Positive Atheism, a moral flaw.

Positive Atheism, as a logical theory, has no possible standpoint. As a practical fact, it is quite as possible as satanic or immoral men. Here, we speak at a disadvantage.

In one respect the tables are turned now-a-days. Formerly men only wrote after patient study and mature thought. At least they spoke respectfully of what they did not understand. Now, a multitude of fools are scarcely students before they are scribblers, and the greater their ignorance, the more gross is the insolence of their denial. It is a mark of genius, now, not to know that two and two make four. It is a proof of "Original Thought" to explain the dictate of Conscience as a mere sort of Molecular movement. Now, a man is honoured as a prophet of "The Age," should he refuse any real praise to virtue, and inflict no real blame on vice. Formerly, honest men might call a spade a spade, blasphemy a crime, and immorality a sin. Now, we are expected to be civil to brutes that preach "Free-Love," and to beg pardon of Atheists for daring to disagree with them. Now, newspapers are covered with criminal detail; reviews are filled with rabid rant; pictures of shameless sensuality are copied into illustrated journals for boys to gaze on; novels planned to describe and glorify lust are thrust into the hands of girls; yet, if we defend our belief in God, we are held to be bigots. If we stigmatise licentiousness, we are ascetics. If we call a spade a spade, there is a shriek of horror from the demi-monde of literature. On the other hand, all that has always been held by all men to be most solemn in truth and most sacred in conduct, is pelted with words gathered from the gutter, and besmeared with metaphor drawn from wanton familiarity with filth.

Bah! If there be any honesty in us, let us stand by truth, and give the lie to falsehood. If there be any honour in us, let us love good, and loathe evil. Let falsehood be challenged, seized, torn to pieces, trampled upon. Let vice be unmasked, struck, flung down, hurled below, damned. Call a spade a spade; an enemy of God an Atheist; a foul man a brute.

A fact is a fact. We must call a hateful fact by hateful names, if we are to speak of it truly. That mawkish way of veneering sin with pretty titles is treason both against truth and virtue.

It is a fact that some men are Atheists, not from conviction but from crime.

Whoever has met with men steeped in foul sin, that was not the outcome of mere weakness, nor even of mere animal degradation, but the deliberate result of bestial instincts fattened, cherished, trained, excited, yet controlled with scientific crime, will have thoroughly understood why these men hate God. He will not have wondered, even while he shrank in disgust, as he saw the actual froth of rabid rage form upon the lips of these human dogs, at the sight or sound of something sacred. Or, whoever has looked into the cold, callous, cynical, satanic eyes of a professional enemy of God, will remember ever afterwards to have seen a physical demonstration of the existence of the devil.

These men, brutes or friends, are out of court. They are absolutely without authority. Nay! rather, their denial, taken with their life, is a proof that God exists. They want wickedness. Therefore, they do not want God. For the sake of decency, if not of self-respect, they are forced to invent a principle that will palliate, if it cannot justify, their practice. Some few of them, indeed, have cast off every covering of shame; but most of them like to have some sort of cloak for their sin. Therefore, they affect to believe that they disbelieve,

"*Si personne ne nie les mathématiques, C'est que personne n'a intérêt a les nier.*" All the wishes, hopes, and fears of these people are set in one strong current against the idea of God. Men who are the thralls of passion, will not submit to God. They cannot manage two masters; so they try to get rid of one. Men whose lives are a flagrant violation of every code of human conduct, have a great objection to the thought of hell. "The wish is father to the thought." The error of their head comes from the evil of their heart. *C'est le coeur qui leur fait mal à la tête.* Once for all, these men are beyond the touch or thought of truth. When they deny God, they lie to others, as they lie to themselves. There is no hope for them, unless they first mend their ways. When they pull themselves together, get married, and settle down to a steady, sober, straight life, they find no difficulty in religion. We have done with them. We will now speak of Atheists whose minds are fairly open and whose lives are fairly good.

Negative Atheism may come from different causes. Some men are Agnostics because they never think about the matter at all. Others, because their minds are warped through exclusiveness in study so that they never give this question a fair chance. Others, because the Faith of their childhood has failed, or appeared to them to fail when tested by manhood's reason. Others, because, whilst honestly seeking after truth, they have not yet reached the goal of clear Conviction.

Unbelief is not always blameless. It does happen that, more or less consciously, the mind is not allowed to dwell upon the thought of God, lest the logical consequence of Conviction should have to be accepted. Religion exercises a control over conduct, of which wild or wilful men are most impatient. Unbelief, even though it be uneasy, is a much more comfortable state of mind than a belief which, although it be recognised, is disobeyed.

Frequently, however, there is no direct disloyalty against truth. Men whose minds are completely monopolised by fancy, like actors, artists, or musicians; or by pleasure, like racing-men, tipplers, or travellers; or by business, like merchants, steam-stokers or slavies; or by hazard, like politicians, speculators, or swindlers, are little likely to think deeply about God, in the hurry, bustle, absorbing excitement, and whirling frenzy of their active hours, or in the stupor of their repose. Yet, at times, the thought of God will force itself upon them, and, if they meet it fairly, they come, in their own way and in their own measure, to the knowledge of his Kingship, to trust in His protection, and to reverence for His law.

In some men's minds, science becomes antagonistic to religion, not on account of any argument, but because "it renders the soil unfit for it!" Can this be possible? Certainly, if a material science, like a loosened wheel, flies spinning out of its proper place. Science is an ordered system of knowledge. Therefore, there is harmony; therefore, subordination, among the sciences. The first and most fundamental science is that which takes the widest possible view of truth, starts from the faintest beginning of certainty, and reaches to the further end of reason. This is the science which treats, not of this particular sort of thing only, nor merely of that other definite kind of thing but of Thing itself. Now, Thing may be considered absolutely as it is in itself, and as it is or may be real, which is the object of Metaphysics;

or, Thing may be considered in its relation to thought and as truth to be accurately imaged, which is the object of Logic; or, Thing may be considered in its relation to will, and as good to be rightly reached, which is the object of Ethics. These are the only universal sciences. The object of each other science is a certain kind of thing, viewed under a certain narrower aspect. Thus, Mathematics only knows quantity. Other sciences only know quality. It is plain that the more universal sciences give light and furnish principles to narrower and more superficial sciences. It is plain, too, that the knowledge of a higher science must be, of its own nature, a direct help to the knowledge of a lesser science. It does not, of necessity, follow that the knowledge of a lesser science is a help to the knowledge of a higher. Nay, if the knowledge of a lesser science bring with it, as it often does, a tendency to judge of truth exclusively from its own narrow point of view, it will lead the mind altogether astray when it wanders into matters that are quite beyond its ken. A higher science can accurately see not only its own object, but the objects, also, of sciences beneath itself. Who sees more, can see less. Who sees less, does not therefore, see more. Again, exclusive development of one faculty, like exclusive development of one limb, does not make a man, but a monster. Tailors have generally nimble fingers, but wretched legs. A first class scholar in Physics or Chemistry may flounder most deplorably if he tumble into Theology or Political Economy. All depends upon whether he set himself to learn in the right way, or not. Should he keep to his weights and measures, to his tubes and retorts; should he want to find out the Co-efficient of Revelation, or the specific heat of honour; should he try to touch the soul with a dissecting knife; or, should he querulously insist on having a definite presentation of God; he will act precisely as some scientific professors do, when they change their lectures on light into sermons on impenetrable gloom. But, if, when his brains have been trained by physical research, and cultured by lessons in art, he is willing to set himself, with the humility of an earnest and honest student, to higher studies in a higher way, all that he already knows will be as a solid stepping-stone from which he can mount securely up to a sphere still more sublime.

A Faith that is not grounded upon reason, may be symmetrical in teaching and admirable in act; but, it can give no more support to conviction than floating clouds, nor to men's aspirations more substance than a dream. Should one have learned in childhood, from teachers that were sincere, a Religion beautiful in many ways but baseless; or, should one's belief in a logically solid Faith have remained always in the same stage of child-like acceptance, nor ever developed into manly understanding; a day may come when he who is a man in all things else, a child in Theology, is led by chance, or forced by argument, into exploring the foundations of his spiritual life. What wonder that a false Faith should crumble at his reason's touch! What wonder even should a true Faith seem to rest merely upon empty air, when childish eyes, peering doubtfully through the twilight of unaccustomed research, fail to notice the spanning arches which give to the whole fabric a fixity and strength like the pillars of Heaven! So, it comes to pass that some men in reasoning about Religion, shrink back dismayed when the structure seems to totter. Henceforth, they distrust their Faith, and insensibly it lifts itself from out of their daily lives and floats afar to distant doubt, like mists that hang about the mountains. Other men wish to know the worst at once. Then, the flimsy fabric of a Faith not grounded upon reason falls with a crash, leaving them blinded and stunned by the dust and ruin of the only Religion that they knew. So, they sit down sadly amidst the broken heaps and shattered walls of that intellectual home wherein their souls had dwelt for years in happy peace; or they wander out into the darkness, not heeding whither they turn their steps. This is not logical. But, men do not easily distinguish between matters, which they have always seen together, and he who has been deceived, or who fancies that he has been deceived, is likely to fling out the true together with the false. Again, a loss that takes place within the innermost sanctuary of conviction and feeling, casts a gloom upon the mind and a chill upon the heart. We must never be ungentle towards the sad; but, with wide patience and deep sympathy, wait and watch by the sick soul for the signs of returning strength. It is, indeed, hard to restore a healthy and genial tone of thought to the mind of a man, who has once turned away, in hopeless regret, from the tomb of a dead Faith. Still, while there is life, there is hope. No one, indeed, can reasonably expect to find the truth in Religion, if he bury himself under a heap of research or exhaust himself in endless analysis. Each one must wisely rest content with such certainty, broadly human, or finely philosophical, as is suited to his own capacity and circumstance. Above all, he must advance with sure and simple steps that bring him forward in one straight logical line. The first step is the Existence of God. The second step is the Existence of a Revelation through the Christ. The third step is the Existence of a Church in which that Revelation is contained. When these three points have been secured, a more subtle and more scientific study of the inmost reasons and relations of things will find a fitting place in vastly varying degree. Questions about the nature of God, about the duty of men, about theoretic side-issues, or about practical detail, can always be best answered, and often can only be answered, when reason's dim and feeble thought is aided by the light of Heaven. For, few men have the time, ability, or patience to become, by elaborate research and philosophic insight, masters of the wisdom of the world.

Lastly, there are men who do not doubt, but who wish, as men should wish, to be able to render a reason for the Faith that is in them. They cannot miss the truth; for, they know where to look for it. All who, without passion and without prejudice, with clear mind and early eagerness, arise to seek for Wisdom "shall find her sitting at their gates."

What has been said appears ample answer to the difficulty; "If the existence of God is evident, how do you account for Atheists?" Putting aside those who sin against the light by criminal revolt or by irrational denial, there are left, those who deny, not the God of reality, but a goblin of their own brain; those who get bewildered over questions, not of existence, but of kind; those whose doubts are mere misgivings, to be easily dispelled; and those who are said to be in doubt because they only see the glimmering of the dawn.

We will here quote the words of two men who have always been held to be wise amongst the wise. Plato says: "No one, even of those who picked up that idea about the non-existence of the Gods in youth, has ever held to that opinion in old age." Seneca says: "They lie who say they think there is no God. For, though by day they may tell thee so; yet, by night and when alone they doubt it." We will add a word from one whom Englishmen at least honour as a deep thinker. "I had rather believe all the fables in the legends of the Thalmud and of the Alcoran, than that this universal frame is without a mind. Therefore, God never wrought miracles to convince Atheism, because His ordinary works convince it. It is true that a little Philosophy inclineth man's mind to Atheism, but depth in philosophy bringeth men's minds about to Religion. Against Atheism the very savages take part with the subtlest philosophers. Among the causes of Atheism are learned times, especially with peace and prosperity; for, troubles and adversity do more bow men's minds to Religion." (Bacon, Essays, Wisdom of the Ancients. XVI. Of Atheism.) So, too, it is written: "Jeshuron waxed fat and kicked: Thou art waxen fat, thou art grown thick, thou art covered with fatness: Then, he forsook God, which made him, and lightly esteemed the Rock of his salvation." (Deut. XXXII., 15.)

SECTION 2. MENTAL ATTITUDES TOWARDS TRUTH

When one has to deal, not with direct and immediate evidence, but with subjects that need long and abstract study, the method and manner of approaching the question, is much more important than the intensity of one's attention or the thoroughness of one's work. Our knowledge can only come to us by bits; it can never come unless each separate fragment that has been gathered, be aptly joined to all the others, so as to form the strongly welded and exquisitely finished unity of science. Rather, knowledge is a vital growth. Unless it spring from healthy roots and gradually build itself up with solid stem, it will not bear intellectual flower or practical fruit.

The soil must be suited to the seed of knowledge. Truth is itself most fruitful; but its action on our mind will depend on the state in which it finds us. Upon our mental attitude towards it, depends whether Truth come to us as a friend or as a foe. If we are honest, straightforward, humble, docile, reverent, Truth will easily enter and dwell peacefully within the home of our thought. But if we are silly, conceited, arrogant, or cynical, either Truth will hold aloof from us, or it must break its way in, and keep us violently bound until we manage to escape from it. All men say that they are the friends of Truth. Yet some men are its hidden enemies. All men say that they are always open-minded towards Truth, yet some listen like peevish children or crotchety old-maids, like eccentric invalids or intellectual rowdies. Before we enter upon a question in which pride and passion have an immense interest, we had better examine the character and credentials of some who glibly seek to settle it. This consideration may also very usefully force us back upon ourselves, and show us whether our own attitude towards Truth be such as it ought to be.

There are grown-up children who petulantly refuse to have anything to do with Truth except in so far as, like a sweet-meat or a doll, it appeals to their coarser senses. One bold boy declared that he had never been able to discover a soul with his dissecting-knife; — exactly the way in which a sulky youth would formulate his disbelief in anything more spiritual than pie or marbles. Another, in whom, as in a girl, love of colour leads fancy to finer flights, pettishly objects to being asked to admit any truth unless a definite picture of it can be presented to his mind.   There is very little rationality in a baby. It is scarcely more than a small animal, living by instinct and by direct un-sifted sense-perception.   As reason comes more fully into use, a higher light is thrown upon things.   In the matter furnished by the senses, reason finds truths to understand which the senses cannot reach.   Thus, as the mind develops, it learns much more than what a girl can put into pretty pictures or a boy mangle with his tin sword.   It is childish to remain exclusively taken up with those truths or facts which appeal to the eye or stomach.   Intellectual hobblede-hoyhood is a bad time for Philosophy.   As when the down first dawns sufficiently upon the upper lip, to be coloured with cosmetic or to be scraped off with a pen-knife, the indefinite and awkward creature is neither boy nor man; so, when a woolly mass of unspun information gathers in the brain, the over-grown and under-developed thinker is neither a simple child of common-sense nor a scientific student of Philosophy.   In order to shorten, if we cannot avoid, the transition-stage from mere common-sense to thorough science, three precautions must be taken.   Firstly, one must never lose hold of common-sense.   Secondly, all intellectual growth must be a living development of Common-sense, without unhealthy off-shoot or morbid excresence.   Thirdly, we must not lean too heavily upon our new science until it is thoroughly seasoned and well tried.   In other words, we must begin by laying down a solid foundation for our knowledge.   It is rather foolish to fix our roof on, before we have walls built to hold it up. Philosophy is the mature age of Common-sense. If you are only a child, be a good child, and use your common-sense. If you are a philosopher, be a true one, and use your reason reasonably. If you are an unfortunate hobbledehoy, be patient, wait, hold your tongue, and learn.

Strutting students make very bad raw material for Philosophy. Their characteristic is conceitedness. Now, conceitedness is the worst possible preparation for study. In the determining of its knowledge, the mind is passive. Truth is not to be coined out of one's own fancy. Invented truth is an absurdity; for it is likeness without an object, knowledge without anything known. Truth acts on the mind, determining, moulding, fashioning, perfecting thought, until thought becomes true, because it becomes the image of thing. If truth do not determine our intellectual life unto living likeness with itself; if truth do not actualise our mind by the gift of its own ideal existence, either we remain in the lethargy of ignorance, or our dreaming brain is weaving the unrealities of error. Truth is to be sought with humble eagerness, to be welcomed with joyful submission, to be obeyed with faithful reverence. This is exactly what conceitedness will never do. The vice of conceitedness, because it knows a little, invents a great deal more. It rattles the coppers in its pocket as if they were guineas. It talks like Solomon, Epictetus, or Ruskin, because it has heard a poetical lecture or skimmed through a fashionable book. A little knowledge lifts the mind up to an unaccustomed height; hence the danger of giddiness. It fills an empty head with the enthusiasm of a strong stimulant; hence, the danger of intoxication. Within the precincts of the lower class of sciences, where matter is taught that is obvious or easily ascertained, a student is not likely to make himself offensively disagreeable by unwarranted dogmatism, because he is conscious that, if he attempt to strut, any ordinary passer-by may knock him over with a fact, or trip him up with a theory. But, there is a great danger of this little knowledge making him unsteady, when he gets into the fresher atmosphere of abstract reasoning. In Mathematics, indeed, he will walk straight if he walk at all, because he is propped up by figures or helped along by lines. But, when his feet are on the slippery slopes of Metaphysics, when, while his brain is fired with the fumes of half-knowledge, he risks, without trusty guide, a perilous ascent to the peaks of Elemental principle, it will be strange if he do not tumble into abysmal error. When young ladies learn to play the piano, or to buy tea, they sometimes consider themselves absolute standards of taste and infallible judges of character. So, too, when conceited students have seen a few amusing experiments and heard a few practical facts, they appear anxious, like children who have got new clothes, to attract notice, and, in order to succeed, they will even strut as dogmatic Agnostics or virulent Atheists. A doctor does not think that, because he knows Medicine, he is entitled to speak with authority on points of law. A judge, even should he have got on the wool-sack, does not consider himself qualified to physic a sick cow. Yet, lack-a-day! all this unruly crowd of uproarious students and intellectual rowdies bursts, with riot and clamour and insolence, into the philosophic shrine where should reign the silence of deep meditation and the solemnity of devout purpose.

We have spoken of those in whom dogmatism takes a

positive shape, and becomes the swaggering self-assertion of a bully. We now come to the other extreme, that in which dogmatism is of the negative and destructive type, rendering the minds which it attacks exclusively critical until at last they lose all healthy appetite for truth. These are dyspeptic spirits. The tendency of modern training is to create an abnormal greediness for mere information, an unwholesome flabbiness of principle, with an inevitable nausea for sound and solid wisdom. The first aim of education seems to be to have students crammed with an undigested mass of facts. Superior education seems to mean that students should be critics. Immature minds are taught to ignore what they cannot deny, to nibble at what they cannot understand, to pick holes in all that they are able to reach. They are not asked to know, much less to prove, what is true in matters of principle. They are asked to learn by rote what others have said, and to point out where these have appeared to fail. Boys and girls, before they are well into their teens, are encouraged to criticise the orchestration of Gounod; the colouring of Tintoret, the character of Hamlet, or the genius of Milton. At a large public examination, little lads were required to give their opinion on Paradise Lost. Horror! Either you suppose the diminutive urchin to be aware of the audacious impudence of such an attempt, or you suppose him to be unaware of it. In the one case, you want the boy to prove himself a brat; in the other case a booby. Boys and girls, before they are well out of their teens, are encouraged to turn their critical eye upon all things human and divine. Having learned a text-book and copied the tone of their grinder, they are, of course, competent to laugh at Aristotle, to pooh-pooh Plato, to sneer at the Schoolmen, to pronounce the grounds of Revelation to be insecure, and to define the existence of God to be incapable of proof.

Now, all this training is not a training for truth, but a training for error. Truth must be treated with friendliness and sympathy, not with suspicion, distrust, or dislike. Therefore, we must not look first for what is false and only afterwards grudgingly admit what is true. Rather, we should first and always look lovingly for the light, and only in the name of truth, challenge error when it comes. If the mind is occupied principally and constantly with error, it will cease to find a relish in truth.

Some men are dyspeptic from their birth. Others get indigestion from unhealthy habits. Just as there are people who will never look one straight in the face, so there are minds that always look askance at truth. But, whether they be crooked by nature or crippled by training, they have got an unhappy twist and suffer from chronic sickishness. They may be intensely stupid, yet, in the matter of fault-finding, they give proof of almost fabulous ingenuity. They are not clever, but they are cunning. They have no talent for truth, but a strange instinct for error. Like vultures that see or smell carrion from afar, they fly past all that is sound, and fasten where there is decay. Utterly incapable, as they are, of appreciating what is beautiful, of reverencing what is true, or of worshipping what is noble, they pass in stolid ignorance where others pause in thoughtful wonder, and discover at once that there is a chip in the pedestal of a statue; that there is a finger-mark on the frame of a master-picture, that there is a comma wanting in a prize-poem, or that a saint was not good-looking.

These creatures have a great power for evil. The atom of truth in their fault-finding is enough to defy denial. They are themselves incapable of taking a fair, full view, of applying a distinction or of admitting an explanation. You may refute their judgment time after time; but, again and again, they will repeat their atom of truth, and then reiterate their sweeping condemnation. Their criticism is true enough to prevent honest folk from giving them the lie direct. Their conclusion is bitter enough to give illnatured men or idle women a venomous joy in advertising it. These intellectual beetles might have their use in the world if they confined themselves to refuse. The misfortune is that they are always ambitious to settle upon the slightest sore part of good and dainty flesh.

Dyspeptic spirits are happy in Philosophy; for, although everything disagrees with them, yet, in it they find ample opportunities for making themselves disagreeable to others. The vastness of Philosophy gives them the widest choice in their search for error. Its vagueness leaves them the easiest chance for escape from truth. When, for instance, a metaphysical proof is brought before them, they recoil in disgust, because it is abstract, abstruse, metaphysical. When a moral proof is offered to them, they contemptuously fling it aside as coarse, unscientific, inconclusive. If you talk Philosophy, they say that they want plain common-sense. If you talk plain Common-sense, they say that they want Philosophy. The only cure for mental dyspepsia is abstemiousness in reading and a habit of quiet well-regulated thought.

There is no need to treat of the mental attitude of those who, more or less consciously, cling to error. In practical life, they are to be shunned. In theoretic discussion, we should either ignore them, or talk to them in pure Saxon.

We have spoken at great length of how we ought not to approach truth. A very few words will be enough to explain what the right dispositions are with which one may be able to answer the great question of all. We should be patient. We should watch daily at the gates of Wisdom. Our intellect depends upon brain-action, and our brain works slowly. The higher the matter of thought, the longer the time required for its thorough assimilation. Again, we must be humble. Truth does not come to the proud, for they falsify its teaching according to their own conceit. But Truth dwells with the lowly, for they appreciate her simplicity and acknowledge her sovereignty. Further we must be docile. We may not rebel against Truth, because our teachers fall short of her perfection. It is foolish to spurn gold because it is given by soiled fingers. We may not sin against the light because it breaks through clouds. Most of all, we should love the light. We should watch for it before the dawn. We should follow it ceaselessly all the day long. We should linger with it still at night-fall, and our heart should dream of its beauty while we slumber. All human worth is in filial acceptance of Truth, in chivalrous allegiance to her sway, and in the sturdy shaping of one's life according to her law.

SECTION 3.   MEANING OF THE QUESTION

We have already explained what is understood by the terms, Being and Existence. We must now make direct and emphatic use of a word which to many minds is mysterious and to some ears offensive. Yet, we must beg pardon of those who dislike it, and ask the patience of those who distrust it, for, there is no other word with the same sterling accuracy or current sense. It is the word, Essence. We wish to bring out the relative meanings of Essence and Existence. Work slowly and cautiously. The notions which we are about to take to pieces and put together again, are most Elementary, yet most abstract, most universal yet most subtle. They require, consequently, delicate and accurate handling.

Essence may be said to be, "That by which a thing is, what it is." Now, a thing is what it is, by that which is most intrinsic to its own identity. Essence is, then, the inmost nature of a thing, its first internal principle of quality, and its most fundamental source of energy. Essence is, indeed, the same thing as Nature but not under the same notion. Essence means the very kind of a thing in relation to its now formal constitution. Nature means that very kind in relation to its outcome of energy or act. Thus, Essence does not mean the external cause by which a thing is made, nor the outside sign by which it may be known, nor even anything within, which is derived result or consequent condition. It is the central self, the intimate own, the innermost kind, by which a thing is constituted its own identical self and nothing other. Essence may be considered under an abstract and metaphysical form, or in its physical and concrete shape. Thus, in metaphysical thought, Humanity is that by which man is man. In physical expression, a man is constituted essentially man by the union of his essential components, soul and body. That we sometimes contemplate things under their abstract essential form is no excuse for the ridiculous accusation that we suppose those essential notions to be realised, under such form, in physical fact. All men talk about Truth and Honour, yet, no man is held to be guilty of saying that Truth and Honour are individuals existing outside truthful and honourable men, because, forsooth, he says that Truth and Honour are realities in the world. Essence, physical or metaphysical, is itself the same, although viewed under different aspects. It is the matter, not the mode of thought, that is affirmed.

Essence may be merely possible, or it may be actual. In one state or the other, it is logically the same. Whether it remain a pure possibility, or whether it be realised in the order of actual things, the Essence is essentially, as far as the notion of it goes, unaltered. That by which Essence is a real fact is its actuality, and this actuality or realisation of Essence is called its existence. Existence is the actuality of Essence.

Everywhere and at every moment, we are confronted with the realised truth, that Essence does not always or of necessity involve its own Existence. If an Essence can, absolutely speaking, be merely possible, it is not of necessity existing. Therefore, such an Essence does not essentially include its own Existence. Your thinking mind was at one time nothing. It was once merely possible. Hence, the essential notion of your mind does not essentially include its own actual Existence. Otherwise, it would be quite as absurd to say that your mind at one time was not a fact, as it would be absurd to say that at one time your mind was not a mind. On the one hand, Essence is as unchangeable as absolute Truth. On the other hand, Existence comes and goes. In other words, Essence may be actual, or it may be non-actual.

Therefore, Essence is not the same logical notion as its own Existence. A Realised Essence is, of course, one and the same physical fact with its own Existence, but, this is not on account of its Essence itself, but on account of the actuality which that Essence happens to have.

Therefore, there is such a thing as Being that is not self-existent. Self-existence is not merely the denial of Existence that is got. It is the affirmation of Existence that is self-owned. Thus, self-existence must mean that a Being is actually existing, just as truly, just as much, and for just the same reason, as it is itself. Therefore, actual existence is as absolutely inseparable from even the logical notion of it, as is the very notion of its identity or of its kind. Self-existent Being is its own actual Existence, in the way in which any Being is its own identical self. Now, all things are not self-existent. For, many things are thinkable as non-existent, although they are not thinkable as not themselves.

Is there a Self-existent Being? This is the first meaning in our question. Our first answer is that there exists a Being whose Existence is not got or given but simply absolutely, and of necessity, owned; an Essence whose Existence is not from without, but from within, not separable, but identical; a Being which exists by itself, of itself, in itself, so as to be, in logical accuracy and in actual reality, its own Existence; a Being so self-existent as to be essentially an impossibility, if it be not essentially a fact.

Is a Self-existent Being, God? This is the further meaning in our question. Our answer is that a Self-existent Being is, in the highest and fullest sense, a Personal God.

Be it, however, remarked, that everything need not be proved at once. We will be quite satisfied with proving, in the first place, that there is a Self-existing Being. We can then go on to prove that the nature of Self-existent Being is such as to be Divine. Again it is not necessary to prove the existence of God as He owns all infinite attributes. It is enough to prove His Existence under any one notion that is applicable to Him alone. Further, remember that difficulties to be met with in the scientific explanation of the nature of a thing, do not disprove its existence. We have, indeed, some very vague idea about its sort when we know a thing to be a fact. But, our certainty as to the existence of a fact need not be shaken because we cannot solve riddles against its kind. Remember, as dear old Aristotle says, "It is a mark of stupidity to abandon a truth on account of difficulties that crop up."

By this distinction between the broad, plain question of the existence of a fact and involved questions about its qualities, its attributes, or its essential kind, the crowd of Atheists is split up into scattered and conflicting groups. Most of them are, in reality, either Pantheists, who hold all things to be parts, fragments, developments, evolutions or manifestations of one self-existent Absolute; or they are Monotheists who believe in an impersonal God, a dead Divinity, a material monster, or a dynamic destiny; or they are Polytheists who admit an infinite multitude of atomic Vulcans, molecular Saturns, or protoplastic Joves.

With regard to the degree of certainty required, it is enough for practical purposes if the proof take away all prudent ground for doubt. It is not necessary that it should exclude the possibility of foolish misgiving. We do not say this as offering any apology for our proofs; but in order to put honest folk on their guard against bumptious boys or boisterous eccentricities who deny a conclusion if they can wriggle out of an argument. There are two ways in which a proof may fail to have effect: one, from a want of power in itself; the other, from a want of perception in its hearer. For instance, a man who slashingly denies common principles of common-sense, who superbly invents principles of his own, who takes his hypothesis for a proof and his fancies for evidence, who coolly sets up his own surmise as an ultimate standard of truth for others, and coolly refuses the intellectual franchise to all minds that dare to disagree with him, such a man may fail to see our proof, not because the proof is not real, nor because the proof is invisible, but because, if he looks at it at all, he does so like one who should judge colour in a London fog or survey scenery through a microscope.

Lastly, mark two facts. Firstly; Against us, there is no proof, only assertion. Secondly; as long as any one of our proofs has not been evidently disproved, our conclusion stands.

Second Book

"I AM WHO AM"

Second Book

"I AM WHO AM"

THE existence of God is so evident, in the order of direct thought, that it may be said to be naturally known. Yet, in the reflex order of thought, where one goes back from the simple spontaneous certainty about things, to a scientific study of their nature, and to an ultimate analysis of their proofs, this truth, like other truths that are almost self-evident, may sometimes become obscured. The change from the clear but superficial view of Common-sense, to the clear insight of Philosophy, must bring its period of difficulty and its peril of doubt. Speaking broadly, the simplest and most evident principles are exactly those which are hardest to absolutely prove. All men, except a few *Cervelles brulées* hold that theft is wrong. But there are scores of contradictory theories as to the ethical grounds for the right of property, and an average man would be unable to answer the objections that might be urged against any one of them. Failure in an attempt to gain a scientific certainty of what we naturally know, is apt to undermine our convictions about such truths as are not constantly forced upon our acceptance by contact with the material world, and thus it happens that the existence of God, however plain to direct thought, may seem uncertain or obscure to the thought that seeks to sift itself.

The way to avoid this danger is not by shirking the

question, but by facing it in the profound calm of meditative leisure, and with the earnest docility of one who really wants to learn.

But, to pass over a philosophic solution with a rush, or to pass it by with a grudge, is far less wise than to rest satisfied with the direct knowledge of common-sense. Some things are better left undone than badly done.

As there is one fundamental relation between the Absolute or Self-Sufficing and the Relative or Dependent, so will there be found one underlying line of reasoning in all the following proofs. In the choice and setting of the actual arguments, the aim has been to bring the deepest principles of world-old wisdom within easy reach of minds of various type and bent. Each reader, may, then, find amongst them all some one at least that strikes his fancy and satisfies his thought.

PROOF I

THE EXISTENCE OF CONTINGENT FACTS IS A REALISED
PROOF OF THE EXISTENCE OF A NECESSARY BEING

CONTINGENT is what happens to be. It need not be a chance, but it cannot be a necessity. When we apply the term to Being, we mean that the Being in question as far as its own nature is concerned, is neither of necessity in the state of Existence nor of necessity in the state of non-Existence. In the most philosophic sense, contingent Being is that which of itself has no logical repugnance to reality, nor of itself anything more than the mere possibility of being made actual. Necessary Being, on the other hand, is that which in its own essence includes an absolute repugnance to the state of non-Existence, which of its own nature cannot be merely possible, but must be thoroughly actual, which cannot get, or receive, nor lose Existence, but which absolutely and essentially is its own Existence. Necessary Being is an immediate contradiction of the possibility of not being. Necessary Being is impossible if it is merely possible. It is impossible unless it exists.

There is no truth that has not some sense in it. The sense that is in it may be seen by itself, or it may require to be proved by a reason drawn from a truth that is higher. There is a final and a sufficient reason somewhere for every truth. What is true of truth is real in reality.

Realities are realised truths. The word "Reason" is used by philosophers not only with regard to the sufficient proving of truth, but also with regard to the sufficient foundation of reality. Every reality must have its sufficient reason. The meaning of this is, that a reality cannot be really real, unless all those conditions are fulfilled which it really presupposes or requires. In this sense the word reason is referred directly to the objective, ontological, actual order of things in themselves. Indirectly and consequently it becomes a reason in the subjective, logical, rational order of things, in the sense that it is the inward strength and life-giving principle of argument. When we speak of a sufficient reason for anything real, we are using the word not in the mere logical sense of truth, but in the ontological sense of ultimate, solid foundation for fact.

Now those who deny the real existence of things, are beyond the reach of argument, as they are beyond the reach of common-sense. If you admit that there is a Necessary Being, you admit all that we at present require. For, Necessary Being is Self-existent, and Self-existent Being as we shall easily show hereafter, is God. If you do not admit that there exists a Necessary Being, you suppose that all things can be contingent. For, there is no possible medium between necessary and contingent; since a thing must either be necessary, or not necessary. If it is not necessary, it is contingent. But it is absolutely impossible that all things should be contingent. Why? Because if all things were contingent, there would be no sufficient reason for their existence. Thus, on the one hand, they exist as we suppose. On the other hand, they do not exist, because they cannot possibly exist without a sufficient reason for

their existence. The most skilful tailor would be unable
to make a coat without any material. There would be
no thought unless there was a mind to think it. If you
never began to walk, there would be little likelihood of
its being true that you had done four miles in an hour.
Why is this? Because the reason for existence is not
sufficient. In other words, nothing is not a sufficient
reason for a reality. How can it be proved that if all
things were contingent there would be no sufficient
reason for their reality? In this way. That sufficient
reason should be realised, either in nothing, which is
absurd; or in something else outside all these contingent
Beings, which you have denied in denying the Existence
of Necessary Being; or, finally, these contingent Beings
would have a sufficient reason for themselves in themselves. This last supposition is also absurd. Let us
make this clear. That sufficient reason could not be in
one single Contingent Being: firstly, in that case such a
Being would be a sufficient reason for itself, seeing that
it is one of the contingent Beings for whom a sufficient
reason is sought. But a Contingent Being which is a
sufficient reason for itself is at the same time a Necessary
Being, because it is self-existent. Thus it would be a
contingent Being that is not Contingent. Secondly,
that Contingent Being like all the others is essentially
non-existent of itself.

Again, the sufficient reason for the real existence of
the world cannot exist in several or all Contingent Beings
if we take them individually. This would be only
indefinitely multiplying the absurd statement that a
Contingent Being can be Self-existent. For, it would
come to this, that either each Contingent Being was a
self-sufficient reason for itself, and therefore self-existent,

and therefore necessary; or it would come to the still more ridiculous assertion that a Being which has no Existence of itself can be final, absolute, supreme, and sufficient reason for the real existence of something else.

Now let us throw a little light into the only corner where an Atheist could lurk. Can the sufficient reason for the real Existence of the world be found in the whole collection of Contingent Beings? No! not any more than a universe of stones could teach a problem of Euclid. One stone cannot talk. The more stones you get together the less chance there is of your coaxing them to speak. It is not in the nature of a stone to speak, and all stones have got the same essential nature. Now it is of the very Essence of Contingent Being to be utterly and absolutely of itself non-Existent. It cannot advance beyond one mathematical point towards its own reality. It has not in the faintest manner, or in the most infinitesimal degree, any share however incipient in its own realisation; nor has it any hold however partial on its own actuality.

Thus, Contingent Being is Contingent. You may multiply it as you will, but the notion is the same and essentially excludes any sufficiency of reason for its own existence. Again, the collection cannot give a sufficient reason. The collection is in reality nothing more than the individuals themselves. Each and every Contingent Being is of itself non-Existent, all Contingent Beings are of themselves non-Existent. The whole collection of them is really nothing more than what they are themselves.

Furthermore if we take the whole collection of Contingent Beings as it makes up one solid, harmonious, and inter-dependent Universe, we are still exactly at the same point of clear evidence. Is the Universe contingent or not? If not contingent, it is necessary. If necessary, its non-existence would be a logical contradiction, a palpable absurdity. But as a matter of fact, the whole Universe of this world might just as well not exist as far as the logical laws of thought are concerned. As far as it is itself concerned, the notion of its nature, or the character of its Essence does not include the reality of its Existence. That it does now exist is a contingent fact, therefore the Universe of Contingent Beings is itself contingent. Therefore it needs a sufficient reason for the reality of its existence which it has not of itself.

Yet again, the collection of Contingent Beings logically presupposes these Contingent Beings. Therefore, in logical priority the sufficient reason for the real existence of the contingent individuals must be realised before the collection itself can have any sufficient reason. But what logically presupposes something else, cannot logically, much less really, be a sufficient reason for it. It is well to bear in mind that we are speaking of what is first and fundamental in reality. One man may be a butcher, another a baker, another a tailor, another a thief, another a policeman, another a statesman, another a clown; and thus they may mutually give and take, and thus they may form the social world. But they cannot be all one another's father, you must give them existence at least to start with before they can help one another. It is not easy for men who have got no money, and no credit, to make one another rich. Contingent Being has no existence whatever of itself. If you want to find a sufficient reason for the real existence which it really has, it would be childish of you to go to another Contingent Being that is exactly in the same plight.

Wherefore all things cannot be contingent. Things that are contingent have a sufficient reason somewhere for their reality. They cannot have it in nothing, they cannot have it in themselves, they must then have it in some being that is necessary. Wherefore the real existence of contingent facts is a realised truth which proves the real existence of a necessary Being. Contingent facts are real consequences following on the condition, that a Necessary Being really exists. The consequences are realised. The condition then must be real.

Let us get right in front of the fact. The world really is. What is the reason of it? Has it none? To assert that there is no sufficient reason for the world, is to identify something with nothing. To maintain that we can know nothing about it, is not only a denial of all Philosophy, it is an abdication of common-sense. To answer that in the Actual Existence of the world there is sufficient explanation of its Being, is to give this childish solution, "It is, because it is." But this is merely an obstinate reassertion of a fact, with an unfair refusal of proof. An Agnostic way out of the difficulty is to declare that there appears no ground for rational belief other than the necessity inherent in the fact. Yet this necessity is consequent on the fact; that is to say, it follows from the fact, and therefore it is no reason for the fact, but the fact is the reason for it. As this necessity is consequent, it is hypothetical, that is to say, it depends on the contingency of the fact. Now, it is exactly this contingency, the fact of a fact being realised although of its own self and in virtue of its own nature, it may or may not be actual, this fact it is exactly that we want a sufficient reason for.

When you say that it is sufficient reason for itself,

you are really saying, "There is no further reason needed, because, as the world really does exist, it must exist." In other words you are saying, "If it is, it is." Remark, however, that you are making three difficulties for yourself instead of one. Firstly, you hold that the logical sequence here is absolutely true, that from your Condition "If it is" must follow your Conclusion, "It is." Now, you cannot explain this absolute necessity of truth, unless you admit an absolute necessity of Being, that is to say, unless you admit that there is a Being, Absolute, Self-existent, and Necessary. This will be more fully shown later. Secondly, what about your Condition "If?" How do you explain the very possibility of it? Certainly not without some sufficient foundation in reality. But Contingent reality is no sufficient explanation for the intrinsic nature of things, since this is prior to and independent of what is only Contingent. Thirdly, you have still, in your conclusion, "It is," the same old difficulty staring you in the face. What sufficient reason is there for the actual realisation of what is of itself merely possible? If you can get no better ground for the Universe of reality and of truth, than a contingent foundation, you can get nothing more than contingency. You can have no necessity whatsoever. There is no reality in your facts. There is no logic in your reasons. You cannot separate what is, from what is not. You cannot divide truth from falsehood. You have no necessity, because you have rooted everything in contingency. There must then be some necessity somewhere. There must be some necessity that is real. But a necessity that is real cannot ultimately rest on a mere hypothesis, on a mere supposition, on a mere condition. Thus, there must be some real foundation for fact and for truth, so necessary as to be absolute and self-existent. Such real foundation must be a Self-existent and Absolute Reality. A Self-existent and Absolute Reality is a necessary Being. Hence facts that are contingent are realised proofs of the existence of a Being that is Necessary.

PROOF II

THE PRINCIPLE OF CAUSALITY PROVES THE EXISTENCE OF GOD

WE wish, as far as possible, to avoid the use of big words. Sometimes, however, a big word has a big meaning. It concentrates on one point many rays of knowledge which otherwise could only be got to sparkle separately on the broad surface of a long drawn sentence. Again, simple words which express simple thoughts are wont to be taken in different senses, and, as ordinary people are the makers of ordinary language, common words become very much tied up with common ideas, so that an easy word that once was the echo of a noble truth falls gradually into a free and easy application, if it does not get quite lost by vulgar usage. When a word was taken from some language that is dead, having upon it the stamp of the changeless past, its meaning is fixed, its message final. As it does not descend to every-day life, it is not subject to wear and tear, nor is it exposed to the soils and stains of rough-and-ready work. The Principle of Causality has a meaning so simple that it is not easy to give it in simple English words. A principle is the beginning, the head, the fount, the source, from which anything proceeds. A principle of truth is that whence knowledge comes. Thus in every science we can retrace our steps from the full flood of masterful information where we stand, back to the tiny rivulets of truths, where this science first springs forth from deeper wells of certainty. Thus, again, we can dig to the first foundations of all proof until we come to some strong evidence that can stand by its own unsupported power. It is in this sense that the Principle of Causality is said to be a principle. It is a first and fundamental truth. It is the fruitful parent of proof.

Causality is an abstract word which means the power of causing, the faculty by which anything is really a Cause, the inherent quality in virtue of which action is exerted. When work is done an effect is produced. An effect is the result of an action. An action comes from a cause. The activity of a cause in relation to its effect, is called its causality. Hence a cause is a principle. But principle has a wider range than cause. A principle is that from which anything proceeds. A cause is also this, but it includes something more; namely, that there is a real difference, a real distinction between the source and the result. Further, cause is usually applied to what is physical; principle is more often referred to what is intellectual. Yet a cause is truly a principle.

The Principle of Causality may therefore be rendered into some such simple words as these.

A fountain-truth is this, that there are fountain-facts. As in the ideal order, there is no truth that does not either come from the evidence of a parent truth, or that is not first mother of its own evidence, so in the real order, there is no fact that is not either Self-existent, or that does not owe its real Existence to the real action of some other real fact. Wherefore it is one of the foundations of logical truth, that a fact which is not first and independent is derived and caused. The

philosophers who have denied or doubted the reality of
the world are of course against us here. However this is
not the place to attack them. We leave them to the
mercy of common-sense. Indeed it is scarcely worth
while to attack them at all. Such difficulties as theirs
are to be met not with the onset of argument, but with
the simple showing of the force of truth. With regard
to the crowd of philosophers who, in England especially,
stick to the judgment of their sense in sober life, yet
suspect the judgment of their intellect in scientific study,
we may pen them into three classes. First, there is the
herd of thorough Materialists, we can let them graze,
they are not likely to do any harm to anybody who is
not already fit to herd with them. Secondly, there are
the half Materialists who ignore rather than deny what
is super-sensible. This class is composed principally of
sheep-like students that rush outside their proper field
in the track of some wild scientist. Neither need we
mind them. If their life is good, they will grow wise
under the teaching of sorrow or with the experience of
age. The third class is made up of men, who, being
unable to explain the origin of our ideas, hesitate to admit
the accuracy or the fullness of our knowledge of the
outside world. At present we can only offer them a
hint as to the solution. We take it that the knowledge
of our senses is true as far as it goes. In that knowledge
is materially contained more than is formally known by
the senses. When the soul, in which are the twin
faculties of sense and intellect, knows an object by one
faculty, it is, thereby, sufficiently determined to turn all
the vision and energy of its other faculty, that this may
also grasp and examine the same object with its own
distinct and higher powers. That this is so, will be

made more plain if we remember that knowledgeable faculties are not free agents. When it is possible that they should act, they must act. Now it is possible that they should act, when on the one hand, their proper object is fitly present to them, and on the other hand, their own energy is sufficiently determined to bear the fruit of actual knowledge. The objects of sense-faculties are made present to them through the medium of physical action. They are sufficiently determined to act, by the vital reaction within them, consequent on their object's action. Our intellectual faculty is determined to act, by the sympathetic influence within itself which results from the fact of the soul's being determined through the medium of another faculty, to actual living knowledge of an object. The object is made present to the intellect, remotely by its presence in the senses, immediately by the spiritual sight of the mind itself. When the soul sees an object by sense, it must also see it by thought. There is this great difference, that sense is passive, concrete, material; thought is spiritual, abstract, active.

As to the Principle of Causality, sense perceives the outward signs of real change, and of real succession. The intellect recognises the truth of all that the senses tell it; but it sees through the reality of the facts, into the very reasons for them. Thus it knows that there is a sufficient reason for everything. It knows that nothing is no sufficient reason for something. It knows that a reality which did not exist before, must have got its reality from something real, it knows the truth, and recognises the application of the Principle of Causality.

At last we have the ground ready for our argument, All things are not effects. There must be a First Cause. If all things that are, have been produced, if there is no

Being unproduced, if there is no First Cause, then we must either conclude that all things are effects, which owe their first origin to nothing, or, we must take refuge behind an infinite series which had no beginning. The first is to deny the Principle of Causality. The second is to try to solve the difficulty by an infinite multiplication of it. We do not deny the absolute possibility of an infinite series. We do deny the possibility of its weakening our proof. If the first effect which we come across must have been caused by something existing before it, have we got a sufficient reason for its reality? No, but we have got now two effects to account for instead of one, because this second reality which is brought in, must have been also produced by something previously existing. Thus as we get to a third, and a fourth, and so on, we are no nearer to any sufficient and final explanation of real Causality, while we have increased infinitely the multitude of real effects which need such sufficient reason. Even if we cannot count back, one by one, the links of this endless chain, yet we can by thought, which reaches beyond space and time, take with one grasp of intellect the whole of this infinite series, and question whether it be real or no. It certainly is not real if it have really no sufficient cause. But a series of which each member is a produced effect, is no sufficient reason for the transplanting of that whole series from empty chaos into actual fact. The whole series itself, made up as it is of individuals, that are each one and all dependent on something else for their existence, depends essentially upon the energy of a Cause, which, as it is the ultimate answer in argument, is therefore the first origin of fact.

Mark well, that this subordination in Causality, by

which all the Causes which we see around us, essentially
depend upon some other agency, is not merely due to
chance or accident but is inherent in the very nature of
things.   Thus, if the action of the first Cause does not
take place, no other action can follow from Causes which
cannot act unless they have been themselves first produced by the action of the first; in other words, that
infinite series of effects is not merely made up of individual units which have been produced, but it is itself, as
is each one of its members, naturally and essentially a
power that is received, an energy that is acquired, a
reality that has been made.   The force of this argument
may be heightened by reference to such effects as have
no sufficient Cause in the material agents from which
they apparently come.   For instance, our spiritual soul
cannot have been made by the material action of our
parents.   It must therefore owe its being to some
higher Cause.   Again, there are very few, even among
Materialists, who do not admit that there was not
always life on earth.   Now either it is granted that
there is a necessary connection between Cause and
Effect, or this is denied.   If it is denied there is no use
in any infinite series, because all the foundations of real
science are swept away.   If it is granted, then, either
you are quibbling, or you recognise that no effect can
surpass the efficacy of its Cause.   The power of a Cause
cannot exceed its own nature.   Its energy cannot exceed
its power.   Its action cannot exceed its energy.   Its
result cannot exceed its action.

We have spoken before of the difference, which there
is between causes which are only accidentally subordi-
nated, and causes which have a subordination that is
essential.   Causes which are also themselves produced

Effects, essentially depend upon a first Cause. Even were it possible that eggs and hens had succeeded one another through an infinite eternity, yet it is utterly impossible that an infinite multitude of eternal wheels should eternally revolve unless there was, or is, something to set them going. It is childish to say that wheel A was set going by wheel B, wheel B by wheel C, and so on to always. Humbug! they are not going at all, or there was something to set them going.

PROOF III

THE EXISTENCE OF POTENTIAL AND DETERMINABLE
REALITIES PROVES THE EXISTENCE OF A BEING THAT
IS SIMPLY AND SOLELY ACTIVE

CHANGE is constant in the world. Where change is
not actual in this universe, it is possible. All that is
not Essential may change. Where there is no real
identity, or absolute connection, not only distinction
exists, but separation may come. Change is the passing from one state to another. The previous state has
passed away into nothingness: the new state begins to
really be. The new state of things did not exist before:
otherwise it would not be new. Before it existed it
was potential. It may be said to have previously existed in the activity of the Cause by which it was produced. If that Cause was simply and solely active, we
have got to the fountain head of activity, and to the
ultimate explanation of potentiality and of change.
For, such a cause would be perfectly independent of all
outside aid, and would need no determining power to
move it from potentiality into act. But should that
cause be itself potential, should it require help from
outside, should its energy be only adequately exercised
through a determination received from something else,
then we must look for a deeper reason, and search for a
nobler cause. That which determines another is actual.

That which is determined by another is potential. Now the actual is more true, more real, more noble, than the potential: because it is further removed from nothingness, and involves more perfect Being. But this Being if determinable must be determined by something more actual, and therefore in this respect greater than itself. In this investigation of determining power, in the universe, in the looking for the mainspring of actuality, we are getting deeper under the surface of things, and closer to the inmost origin of change. We get thus far; each and everything that acts on others, determining their potential power to become realised in act, while it is yet itself potential, changeable, determinable, each and every such thing can only be itself realised or brought into action, if there be given a higher power to bestow upon it an actuality which it has not got itself. For these relations of inter-dependence cannot be all in the same sphere. There are relations of interchanging action amongst beings that are equal. But these relations are not equal in the same respect, and the superiority of what is actual over what is potential must in its own line be grounded upon a reason and a reality rooted in a more fundamental order of existence. Thus my will may determine my feelings, or my feelings may determine my will; but the determination which comes from will springs from the determination of thought, and that from the determination of truth: and that from the determination of absolute necessity. The determination which comes from feeling is determined successively by more and more fundamental agencies of the physical world. Now, as in the intellectual world there is a wonderful symmetry and unity of truth, so, in the physical universe there is an admirable proportion and oneness of order. The lesser laws, which are the expression of the surface forces of matter, lead to higher laws which are the formulas of deeper powers. Science is only searching at present. It has found a great deal of order, and as it approaches perfection it finds greater simplicity. It has visions of unity, although it has not found it yet. How is it that all order brings us back to unity? How is it that all laws trace their power up to the simplicity of a principle? How is it that all determining action borrows its impulse from some superior power? How is it that all change supposes something unchangeable? It is because what is potential and dependent must receive from another the activity and the impulse which it has not got itself. This process of dependence cannot be indefinite; for then it would not be real. It cannot be infinite; for then it would be endless, and therefore could never have begun. It must be finite. It must get to the bottom of reality, and it must touch the summit of truth. Thus, it must be founded upon the existence of a Being that needs no determination, because it is purely active; that can suffer no change, because it is purely perfect; that needs no further reason, because it is final truth; that requires no previous reality, because it is absolutely the First Fact.

PROOF IV

WE are entering on an argument which may be taken, as it is often given, in a false sense, or which may be taken in a sense that is sound. Saint Anselm was the first to make this proof popular. His proof is as follows: "That, than which nothing greater can be conceived, exists. God is such a Being. Therefore God exists." That the greatest conceivable being is God, Saint Anselm does not prove, because it is involved in our very notion of the Godhead. That such a being exists, Saint Anselm proves by remarking that if existence does not belong to such a being, we fall into the contradiction of saying that a being than which nothing greater can exist is without the greatest of all prerogatives, namely, actual existence.

Descartes puts this proof in another way: "Whatever is involved in the notion of Anything must be affirmed of it. Now, Actual Existence is involved in the notion of God. Therefore actual existence must be affirmed of Him."

The most pointed and powerful setting of this argument appears to be that of Leibnitz: "God is possible, therefore He exists." The possibility of God is more evident than the possibility of anything else. That the actual existence of God may be deduced from His possibility, is apparent from the fact that, in the case of Necessary Being, Possibility and Actuality are identical. The faults found with this argument are of two kinds. Firstly, there are difficulties brought against the antecedent in the argument, that is to say, against the principle or ground on which proof rests. Secondly, there are difficulties brought against the sequence, that is to say, against the logical nature of the deduction drawn from the grounds which are given.

The first class of objections is aimed against the assumption that the Existence of God can be proved *a priori*, or *a simultaneo*. This objection is quite valid. To prove the Existence of God, *a priori*, means that the actual Existence of God is proved by the Existence of something prior to God: which means that the actual Existence of God is proved by something which proves that He is not God at all. For if anything can be prior to God, God is not God. To say that the argument is *a simultaneo*, means that actual existence is proved neither by what is prior, nor by what is consequent to it, but by something which, both in order of time, and in logical connection, is simultaneous with it. Now, this may be all very well, if we merely compare God's actual Possibility with God's actual Actuality. This, however, is not the real point to be proved, and consequently it is not from this that the argument should get its name. If you suppose that God is really possible, you may at once conclude, with absolute evidence, that God really exists. But that God is really possible, not merely in your fancy, but in real fact, this is precisely what you have got to prove. This you cannot prove *a simultaneo*; you can and must prove it *a posteriori.* Give up the quaint name. Take the proof itself, and see what it is made of.

The second class of objections against this proof attacks its logical sequence. It is a venerable principle amongst philosophers that proof consists in the revealing of reasons which contain the conclusion, not in the creation of conclusions which were not real before. Proof is an unfolding of reasons. It is not an unreasonable addition imposed upon credulous minds. Hence, there can be nothing in the conclusion of an argument that was not already real, although perchance unknown, in the grounds or principles from which it comes. Whatever is newly added on in argument is a new assertion. It is not a development of proof. It is a petition for belief. With regard to the present question, if in the grounds from which you start, you have nothing more than what belongs to the purely logical world of possibility, you have no right to arrogate to your conclusion, a substantial existence in the world of fact. If you start simply from the logical notion of God's Possibility, you are not justified in claiming for your Conclusion a status amongst physical matter-of-fact truths.

To understand the full bearing of this on our subject, we must remember that when we speak of actual existence, the whole matter of our thoughts may have only such reality as belongs to the ideal world, or it may have the reality which belongs to the world outside the mere mental order of truth. Actual Existence may be realised only in logical conception, or it may be realised in downright fact. In the first case existence has only the actuality of intellectual reflection; in the second case existence has the actuality of physical exercise. It is evident that if we can only prove the existence in the first order, we have no right to congratulate ourselves on having proved existence in the second order of things.

That it is perfectly lawful and logical to pass from the order of ideas to the order of facts, no one can doubt. But such transition must be guaranteed by reason, and rest on evident grounds. If it were never possible to conclude from thought to reality, we could never conclude at all; because we cannot argue from one reality to another, except through the medium of things as they exist in our mind. If it were always possible to infer that there is physical fact where there is logical necessity, we should have to admit that mathematical theories are as solid as stones, and as palpable as our own bodies; because their intellectual evidence is absolutely undeniable. Now let us see whether we cannot find a solid and plain proof of God's Existence in actual fact, from the logical evidence of God's Possibility.

In the first place, what do we at present mean by the term God? We mean nothing more than a Being which is necessary, or what comes to the same thing, a Self-existent Being, or again, what is really the same, a Being whose existence is absolutely independent of all other Being. There is no impossibility in such a Being. This appears quite plain. Some may perhaps find it still more simple, if they remark that in the notion of such a Being there are included some few primary ideas which cannot clash. We have the idea of a Being. The truth of this idea is supposed by all other truth. Then we have the idea of Existence. Here we have no repugnance, no logical opposition; for Being and Existence are realised together in every being that exists.

Now we have the notion of Existent Being. If we add the idea of Self-ownership so as to exclude all dependence on others for Existence, so as to include all perfect possession of whatever is required for existence, do we fall into logical contradiction? No! for the added notion is not in itself absurd, nor does it in any way interfere with the notion already prepared.

If Existence can be received, it can be given. If it be given, it can be owned. If it can be owned, there is no absurdity in supposing an Existence which is so thoroughly itself as to be really, as well as logically, identical with itself. If it is really identical with itself, these subordinate ideas of Being and Existence are only different aspects of one true fact which can no more fail to exist than any other Being can fail to be itself. Hence, that Self-existent Being is possible seems to be as evident as it is clear that any Being is possible. If what is subordinate, dependent, hypothetical, is real, then surely, the notions pre-supposed to these notions must be, at least in themselves, possible. In a word, God is possible because there is no logical impossibility involved in the notion of Him. Were there such contradiction it could only be, because Existence and Necessity cannot coalesce. This is evidently untrue. Therefore, God is possible.

This possibility of God's existence is a truth. So far it is real. We know that it is really true. We are conscious of our own real existence. We understand thoroughly that what is evident to us must be in itself true. Therefore we recognise the fact of God's Possibility.

When we say that two and two make four, we may speak in a mere abstract sense, meaning, that if two pairs be added together we should then have four; or, we may speak in a real sense, meaning that there are two pairs actually given, and concluding therefrom that there is an actual four existing. When we speak of the possibility of God, we may remain among the nebulae of logical conceptions, or, we may be firmly connected with Earth. If the Possibility of God is considered simply and solely in itself, it can be, as far as we are concerned, only a logical notion. If it is considered as the necessary judgment of a living intellect, as the developed fruit of actual thought, and as the only possible foundation for an intellectual necessity which is, both true and real, we have a Possibility which brings with it whatever reality is involved in the notion of its non-repugnance.

We do not conclude directly and immediately from the Possibility of God, that He actually exists. Starting from the mere Possibility of God, we conclude His Actual Existence through the medium of the truth of our own thought, and through the medium of the fact of our own reality. Our argument runs in this way: that God is really possible is a truth, the evidence of which actually appears before our mind. Either this evidence is to be taken as the real result and logical proof of facts that are truly mirrored in the mind, or, we must abandon all connection between reality of fact and truth of thought. Now, no adequate reason can correspond in the region of reality to the notion of God's Possibility, except His Own Actual Existence. Beings that are finite cannot have within them a sufficient explanation for a Being that is infinite. The necessary cannot spring from the contingent; nor the absolute from the relative. In other words, that God is possible is an evident truth, which, when we reflect on it, we recognise as something which we must affirm to be a fact. But the possibility of God cannot be a fact unless His actual existence is also a fact. Therefore we must acknowledge that the actual existence of God must be admitted as true.

In this argument we have adopted a line of reasoning which, although it may appear novel and perhaps doubtful, seems to us personally to be perfectly plain and thoroughly true. It is simply to change the *a priori* argument of Leibnitz into an argument *a posteriori*. From the truth of our own thought and from the reality of this world, which are effects and results of God's Existence, we prove, without supposing it, God's Possibility. Then directly and immediately we conclude God's Existence. For my part, I cannot understand how any rational creature could doubt about the Possibility of Necessary Being. Nor can I understand how any one who sees that Possibility, can avoid seeing that Necessary Being does actually exist. However it is not right in a matter of this kind, to put forward any arguments which might awake the suspicion of any waverer, or estrange the sympathy of any adherent. We leave the argument as it stands. The idea which it embodies is worth while meditating upon.

PROOF V

THE POSSIBILITY OF ANYTHING PROVES THE EXISTENCE OF GOD

It will be clearer if we begin by indicating the chief points of this proof. Firstly, the whole order of possible things must have a firm foundation in real fact. Secondly, that real fact cannot be the reality of things that are contingent; nor can it be an intellect that is contingent; nor can it be any being that is not intelligent; nor can it be any intellectual being that is finite. Therefore the real fact which is the first source and ultimate explanation of all Possibility is a Being that is Infinite, Intellectual, Absolute, and Self-existent.

That Possibility must have its sufficient reason in a fact that is real, we may prove in this way: Possibility is not mere absolute, empty nothing. Possible beings are distinguishable one from the other. Thus a possible man is not a possible donkey. Again, one possible Being follows from another. Thus from the Possibility of eyes follows the Possibility of a squint. This cannot be said of mere nothingness. Again, possible Beings are positive objects of intellect and will. The intellect cannot change the nature of Possibility. A possible circle forces the mind to admit that it cannot possibly be square. This is not true of absolute nothingness. Again, possible beings may exist. Nothingness certainly cannot.

Now, on the other hand, while Possibility is not mere nothingness, it is not any physical reality. Possible beings cannot be said to have any actual existence. Facts that do exist in this world of ours are subject to time and space, are contingent, and changeable. Their Possibility is above and beyond time and space; it is immutable and necessary. This is so simple that explanation or proof appears to be quite superfluous. If this Earth did not exist at all, it would nevertheless be perfectly possible. Yet, in that case it would not actually exist. Hence, possible beings have not within themselves any actual existence.

But can possible beings be said to have no sort of reality except that which they obtain by becoming actual objects of thought? No. They are not merely possible because we reflect on them. Their Possibility is not created by our mental action. Their nature is independent of our thought. In fact, although a possible Being may acquire from my actual consideration, that reflected light which consists in being thought about, yet it is rather the truth of the possible Being which determines my mind, than that the reality of my mind determines the nature of that possible Being. My mind presupposes its object's truth; and in all truth there is involved either some kind of reality, or some necessary relation to reality. Thus, my mind presupposes in its object, some connection with reality that is independent of my mind. Thus, possible things do not get all their reality from the existence which they may be said to have as objects of actual thought.

We must pause a moment here, in order to gather together three conclusions which we have just proved. Possible beings are not mere nothing. They have no actual existence. They are not real merely because they are actual objects of thought. What are they then? They are logical and necessary truths. Wherefore their sufficient reason must be sought for in the actual existence of some real fact from which arises the logical truth that is in them. Truths that are not facts have no possible reality of their own; but they have that reality which consists in a real relation founded on and arising from a real fact. Therefore, again, the whole order of possible beings must have its sufficient reason in some really existent fact.

What can that fact be? It cannot be anything contingent; for, Possibility is both presupposed by whatever is contingent and is independent of it. Possibility, then, cannot have its sufficient reason in anything contingent; because the sufficient reason for a thing must be prior to it in the relation of natural dependence, as well as in the order of logical supposition. In other words, the sufficient reason for Possibility is that on which the truth and reality of Possibility depend. The reality and truth of Possibility do not depend on anything that depends on them. What is contingent depends on Possibility; because its existence presupposes its Possibility; its Possibility does not presuppose its Existence. Therefore Possibility does not depend on what is Contingent. Therefore the sufficient reason for Possibility is not to be found in anything Contingent.

Can the sufficient reason for Possibility be found in a Being that is real yet not intelligent? No; for the sufficient reason of Possibility must include an adequate explanation for whatsoever is contained within the whole order of possible things. Now, intellectual beings are possible, and, as they are more perfect than unintellectual beings, in no one of the latter can there be a sufficient reason for the former.

Can that Real and Intellectual Being in whom we are to find a sufficient reason for the Possibility of all things that may or may not exist, be a finite Being? No. The order of Possibility is without limit either in quantity or in quality, either in extent or in intensity, either in the multitude of the individuals that are possible, or in the degree of perfection which is possible to them. For all this there must be a proportional foundation in reality, an adequate explanation in fact, a real and sufficient reason. This cannot be realised in anything finite. On the other hand, nothing indefinite can exist. Therefore the real and sufficient reason for the logical order of possible things is only to be found in a reality that is intellectual and infinite. But a reality that is intellectual and infinite is God. Therefore, the order of possible things presupposes, and therefore proves, the reality of God. Therefore God exists.

We may set this proof in another form. Beings whose Possibility and Existence are not really identical and logically inseparable, presuppose a Being whose Possibility and Existence are inseparable and identical. Now, a Being such as this is God. Here is the proof of our first assertion. Beings whose Possibility and Existence are not identical, are Beings whose Possibility is, logically at least, prior to their Existence. Now what is logically prior is a reason for what follows from it, not vice versa. Their Possibility, then, is a reason for their Existence; but not a sufficient reason for it, because this Possibility, itself, requires a reason for itself. Possibility cannot be a sufficient reason for itself, since it is only something logical, — a truth; but everything logical, — all truth must have its sufficient reason in something real, because truth is the image, the reflection, the mirrored relation, the thinkable re-echo, coming from and consequent on reality. Possibility, therefore, must have its sufficient reason in a reality that is prior to the whole order of things that may or may not exist, that is to say, in God.

Briefly: the real order presupposes the logical: — The logical order presupposes the real. Is this an absurd circle? Yes, unless we say: the real order that is contingent presupposes the logical order that is necessary. The logical order presupposes a real order that is necessary, in which the logical and the real are identical and simultaneous; so that, on logical explanation of truth, we get up to the final truth of sufficient reason, as it is the first fountain of real fact.

PROOF VI

THE EXISTENCE OF GOD IS PROVED FROM THE OBJECTIVE STANDARD AND RULE OF JUDGMENT

THE word Nature is often used in a vague and general way to express either the world of material sights and sounds in which poets and painters revel, and in which poor people toil, or the whole world of things that really are. Taken in a particular and exact sense, the nature of a thing properly means "The inmost source and principle of its power."

There is a necessary relation of proportion both in kind and in degree, in sort as well as in measure, between the principle of activity and the action which comes from it, between the resultant effort of energy and the primal source of it. Otherwise, something could come from nothing and nothing could cause something; which would render reality unreal, or make nothing real. This is no play on words. To deny a necessary relation between nature and action, is, logically, to confound fact with chaos; to doubt it, is wilful logical dotage. Such a denial would be a negation of all science. Such a doubt would be an abdication of all Common-sense. Again, there is a like relation, although in an inverse sense, between the possibility of a nature, or the potential, pliable, determinable function of its being, and the actuality which naturally energizes or determines it.

Were a nature thoroughly, in its own sphere and kind, perfect, it would require no outward energy to enable it to act; but in so far as a nature does require a real influence from outside to perfect it, in so far it is passive. When a nature essentially needs, for its own development and perfection, the determining action or the possession of something outside itself, this aim of natural tendency, this end of natural movement, this magnet of natural attraction, this goal of natural desire, may be called that nature's own proper object.

As the same nature may, under different aspects of its own, tend towards objects of different orders, it may be said to have different faculties; for a faculty is the direct and immediate power which a nature has of using its energy in a certain way, or of receiving an influence of a certain kind. Thus, the power which our soul has of being developed and perfected by the determining action of evident truth, is called its intellectual faculty. The power which our soul has of actively making a spiritual movement towards good, is called the faculty of Will.

The object of a faculty may be considered as it is in itself, without reference to that faculty, and merely in its own absolute nature. In this case it is not really considered as an object but as a thing. It may also be considered relatively, as it is really suited to be the particular and special object of that particular and special faculty. In the first case it is called the Material Object. In the second case it is called the Formal Object. As one faculty may, under one formal aspect, be referred to many material objects, widely differing in their own absolute nature; so, one material object may, under different formal relations, be referred to

different faculties. Thus our minds may, by reason
of the truth that is in them, be acted upon by a star or a
rag, by an argument or an apple. Thus, again, an
apple may be the object of a metaphysician's thought,
of a painter's imitation, of a green-grocer's avarice, or
of a school-boy's voracity. It is not by its mere money
value that it racks the metaphysician's brain, nor does
it woo the juvenile stomach by the exquisite curves of
its shape, or the delicate blending of its rich red with
fainter and fairer hues. We are safe in saying that a
material object only acts on a faculty through the formal
object of the latter; in other words, that a thing can
only be the object of a faculty, by reason, and in virtue
of a real relation in it, which formally fits it to act upon
that faculty. Now anything may be a material object
of mind, because there is nothing that is not knowable.
The formal object of the mind is truth, because it is
only in virtue of the truth within it that anything can
be known.

In its judgments about evident truth, the intellect
is passive. The physical act of knowledge is the fruit
of the intellect's vital energy, but the actual conception
which results in this mental birth, the necessity of producing a judgment of a specified kind and character,
this the intellect passively receives from the object.
The intellect does not make truth. It recognises it.
The intellect does not determine what is or is not true.
Its judgments are determined one way or the other by
the specifying influence of the object's truth. The
intellect does not lay down, fix, or establish the law that
guides its own intellectual action. It acknowledges and
obeys a law above itself. The intellect does not legislate
for truth. It judges according to the ruling of truth.

The utterances of intellect are not the measure of truth. Its judgments are determined by the objective standard of truth. This is evident from the very nature of knowledge; for, knowledge is an intellectual likening of the knowing to the known; it is the vital image within the mind of an object that is without. Now, the image is not the rule and standard of the original; but the original is the rule and standard of the image. Wherefore, in the formulating of its judgments, intellect is passive. It receives a real influence, it is determined by a real force which is exercised by objective truth.

The determination of intellectual judgment is not due to the mere material nature of its object. In the first place, an object must be, in a sense, intellectualized before it can act on intellect. In other words, an object's influence must be elevated to an intellectual sphere in order to become an intellectual determination to judgment. How this happens, we need not now enquire. That something of the kind must somehow happen is enough to show that material objects cannot directly and immediately determine judgment. In the second place, as we have explained above, the material object of a faculty only acts on that faculty through and by its formal object.

Again, the determination of intellectual judgment is not sufficiently explained by the intellect's formal object as this exists merely in contingent and passing facts.

Facts, in as far as they are contingent, passing, changeable, and perishable, cannot be the ultimate rule and supreme standard of judgments which can only be determined by absolute and eternal truth. Facts, in as far as they are realised applications of eternal and absolute principles, are existent necessities of truth;

and, in so far, partake of a formal influence to which intellect must yield. But, even in this sense, facts, not being self-existent, have of themselves no absolute necessity and no independent truth. Their necessity is no more than hypothetical. Their truth is no more than a consequence. Hence, intellect while convinced by the necessity of the truth that is in them, is so convinced only in virtue of a truth, the necessity of which is absolute. What is hypothetical essentially presupposes what is absolute. What is dependent essentially presupposes, in logical sequence, that which is independent. Any truth that is a consequence or an application of a higher truth cannot be really true unless the latter in logical priority and in necessary superiority, be first really true. Thus, two pairs of candle-sticks make four candle-sticks, because two and two make four. If the latter principle be not absolutely and eternally true, we can never count our candle-sticks. It is the same principle that is presupposed whether it be a case of candle-sticks or of cabbage-stalks. Therefore it is that the intellect judges of facts, deciding their truth by the light and influence of absolute and eternal necessities of truth. In these supreme and absolute truths have we got the ultimate rule and necessary standard of judgment? Yes: we have in first principles, the ultimate immediate rule and the ultimate formal standard of judgment. For, on the one hand, the evidence of all other truths leans on the evidence of truths that are primal; on the other hand, these primal truths are incapable of proof, because there is no higher principle to lend them light, and they have no need of proof, because there is no possible doubt that can dim their own evidence.

Yet, these first truths need further explanation.
They are, indeed, the formal rule and standard of
judgment; but, they must have a proportioned and
sufficient foundation in reality. We will first make
this clear. Then we may readily understand what
that foundation is. Objective truth, considered in itself,
is a mere logical necessity. That two and two make
four is true independently of its ever being realised in
fact or present to intellect. If it were not so, there
would be no necessity for an actual four to be made
up of two twos, nor would there be an inevitable rule
of the kind to which all judgment should essentially
submit.

This logical necessity is the mere objective abstract
identity which there is between two twos and four. It
is not of itself an actual fact, nor is it of itself an existent
reality. Therefore like all abstract truth, it must have
a proportioned foundation in fact, a sufficient explanation in the order of reality. Now, such foundation and
explanation is not sufficiently supplied by contingent
and temporary facts; for, these are hypothetical and
transitory, first truths are absolutely necessary and
independent of all contingent action, of all time, of all
space. Again, all realised facts essentially presuppose
essential truths of which they are contingent realisations.
Facts, then, that are contingent and only hypothetically
necessary cannot be an adequate foundation for an
explanation of truths which are essentially changeless
and absolutely necessary.

Neither can such sufficient foundation and explanation
be afforded by the nature of the action of intellect.
Nay, rather, the real influence which these truths exercise on intellect, really forcing it to submit, really deciding

its thoughts, really ruling and determining its judgments, proves that they have a real power and virtue which they must derive from some reality. They are abstract, reflected, imaged necessities of the purely logical order. Hence, as they are not realities themselves, they must have an adequate foundation in the order of reality. To attempt to explain all this by the nature of intellect itself would be, in the first place, to contradict all common-sense, which evidently recognises that judgment is a recognition of truth, not a mere fabrication or invention that decides what shall be true. In the second place, it would be a condemnation of all science, since it would found this on subjective mechanism, not on objective evidence. It would even be a self-condemnation of intellect, a mental suicide, a self-asserting knowledge affirming to itself that all knowledge is a self-told lie.

Wherefore the ultimate formal rule and standard of judgment must have a proportioned foundation in fact, a sufficient explanation in the order of reality. Such foundation must be at least logically prior to these truths, because principle is logically prior to its consequence, cause is prior to its result, and so foundation is prior to what follows from, or rests upon it. Such foundation must, as we have seen, be real. Such foundation must be eternal; it must be absolutely independent and absolutely necessary; it must be within itself, and of itself, perfectly self-existent in reality and self-explanatory in truth; it must infinitely identify the logical and real orders, so that, in it, truth does not presuppose reality, nor reality presuppose truth; so that in it, all truth is intrinsically real, and all reality intrinsically true; for it must eternally and ultimately determine truth; it must necessarily and absolutely determine reality.

The intellect judges all things that are contingent, changeable, and dependent, by a rule and a standard that is superior and prior to them all. To that rule the intellect itself must bow. By that standard are all its judgments determined. That rule is inflexible, inexorable, eternal, infinite. That rule is, yet, no real fact itself, although it has a real influence that is a fact. Now, the real influence, in matters of fact, of a rule that is abstract, must be founded upon some real fact, of which that rule is an ideal adumbration, a reflected light, a logical repetition. That real fact, ultimate and adequate foundation of such ideal rule, must be of its own nature prior to that rule, and in itself, must have all that is needed to explain and cause the ideal rule and real influence of which it is the first source, and supreme principle. Such foundation to be the first source, must have all the reality of a fact that is coeternal, and coextensive with absolute truth; and all the necessity of a truth that is coequal, and coexistent with essential reality. It must be a true fact that is eternal, actual, infinite, absolute. It must be a truth essentially self-realised and a fact essentially self-existent. It must be God.

PROOF VII

THE EXISTENCE OF GOD IS PROVED BY THE SUBJECTIVE NATURE OF WILL

THAT each actual human nature has actual limits to its own inherent greatness, there can be no serious doubt. The most poetical of Positivists, or the most "uproarious" of Optimists, would scarcely say that he or she is possessed of absolute and infinite perfection. Sensible people, at least, are well aware that they are after all very insignificant items in the midst of the vast universe. Our nature is decidedly finite. Our faculties are finite, too. For, either they are merely different aspects of our nature, or, even if they be in reality distinct powers which emanate from it, they cannot surpass in perfection the source whence all their reality comes. It is equally evident that our will is not thoroughly self-sufficient. It seeks for something outside itself. It is not, therefore, identical with its own complete and thorough perfection. Whether its own perfection or advantage of whatever kind, be its own end or not, this is clear that as it actually exists in its seeking stage, it is not its own end. If it were actually its own end, it could have no further natural need of anything. As a matter of fact, it has natural needs. It is not, then, its own end.

While our intellect is in itself finite, it can look beyond

the narrow barriers of actual time and space. It can
look beyond the cramped horizons that hem in our
positive existence. It can look towards what is boundless. Now, mind is the measure of will. The only
limit to desire is thought. We cannot love what we do
not know; but we can love any good that we do know.
Our mind and will are finite faculties, but no term can
be set to the objective scope of their power. There is
no limit to knowledge; therefore, there is no limit to the
will's desire; therefore nothing finite can be its adequate
object; therefore, its adequate object must be infinite.
Mark well, that the adequate object of the will is no
indefinite good. It is simply and absolutely infinite.
Intellect can soar above and beyond all finite bounds of
perfection, and, with the grasp of one thought, hold the
idea of an all-perfect good. This thought unveils to
the will an object of infinite attractiveness, to the extent
of whose greatness there can be no stop, in the intensity
of whose goodness there can be no stain. There is no
absurdity in the thought of a perfect Being. Otherwise
there would be an inherent contradiction between perfection and Being; which is downright nonsense. Therefore, as relative Being is possible, so absolute Being is
possible. Therefore, absolute perfection is possible.
Therefore, a Being of absolute perfection is possible.
Therefore, a Being of absolute perfection is a possible
object of thought. Therefore, the objective range of
thought is not simply indefinite, it is infinite. Therefore, the objective scope of will is neither finite, for that
would prove truth to be measurable by a finite scale;
nor indefinite, for that would prove thought to be tied
down to actual concrete objects like sense-perception.
Therefore, the objective scope of will outstrips all bar-

riers of finite good. Therefore no finite perfection is commensurate with the objective impulse of will. Therefore, the will cannot be adequately contented and crowned by any finite good. Therefore, the adequate object of the will is an object that is in itself infinitely and absolutely perfect, and that is reached by the subjectively finite hold of evident knowledge and secure love. Therefore, while the will is a finite faculty, nevertheless, it has within its inmost nature a subjective impulse towards an infinite object. So far, we have remained within the ideal order. We enter now into the order of reality.

Our will is a faculty. It is also a fact. This fact is an essential aptitude, a relative potentiality, an inevitable tendency, an intrinsic need, an actual want, a real movement of our very nature. That, underneath all our free desires or conscious cravings, there is a fundamental impulse which necessitates a real movement of our nature onwards and outwards, no sane man will doubt and no serious man will deny.

In this real movement of our nature, in this essential impulse, there are two things for which there must be a real reason in the order of reality. If they are without real reason, they are without real truth, and therefore without reality. The first thing is the evident kind or sort of this movement; the second is the downright fact of this movement.

As to the kind of this movement, let it be observed that, as our ideas are clothed and coloured by the forms and hues of sense-perception, this word, movement, may either hinder or help us by its metaphor. It would hinder us if we were to regard it as mere metaphor and stop short at the shell without reaching the kernel of

its meaning. Movement means the passing from place
to place. But it may also mean the passing from
potency to perfection; it may mean the passing from a
feebler degree of Being to a fuller; it may mean the
passing from one point to another, not in extent of
space, but in intensity of quality; it may mean an impulse given or received that does not transport from
place to place, but bears onward from a potential starting-point towards a term of more realised actuality.
Understood in this way, the metaphor of movement
will help us; for, while its underlying truth of application will guide our reason, its material figure will aid
our imagination.

Of what sort, then, is the movement of our will? Its
intensity and its extent, its force and range, its velocity
and its momentum, must be measured and recognised
by its formal object. This may be proved both from
the nature of the will, and from the nature of the formal
object. The nature of the will is in its being the faculty
of love, the power of vital appetite, the energy of living
quest for good, the spiritual clasp of good possessed.
The mode and manner in which such a nature works,
will be commensurate with its fundamental need and
primal impulse. Hence, from the essential mode and
characteristic manner of its working, may be measured
the kind and quality of its necessary movement towards
good. But this very mode and manner can be alone
gauged by the formal way in which it tends towards
its term. But the formal way in which it tends towards
its term is to be recognised by what, in the object,
objectively corresponds, as end, aim, crown, and goal,
to the will's potentiality for good. This is the will's
formal object. Again, the nature of the formal object

is in its being the definite and adequate attractive power
definitely and adequately suited to act upon the will's
attractability, and in its being the definite and adequate
term definitely and adequately proportioned to the
will's impulse. It is evident that from the nature of
such power and term we may determine the nature of
the will's movement. Let it not be thought, that in
bringing forward these two arguments, we are begging
the question, proving the nature of will by the object,
and proving the nature of the object by the nature of
the will. No. We are looking at the will's movement,
first from its starting-point; then, from its goal. Both
views help towards a thorough understanding of the
course to be explained. Yet, both arguments do prove.
If, however, any one were to substantially deny the real
nature of will, or the real nature of its formal object,
we should then prove one or the other from independent
grounds. If, on the other hand, as at present we do
suppose to be the case, our reader has any true notion
of will, be it ever so elementary, both arguments stand
steadily by their own weight, and contain deep wells of
truth for the meditative mind.

Now the formal object of will is good, simply and
solely as such. This is a cardinal point of our argument.
Let it be well looked to. The will is not tied down to
one particular kind of good. The object of the eye is
colour, not sound or smell; but the will may seek as its
own that which is the object of any sense. Nay, the
will is not limited to the objects of material powers. It
may love virtue as well as food, science as well as sleep.
Its power, therefore, of love is capable of being directed
towards any possible sort of good. Therefore, that
which formally renders anything formally fit to be the

object of will is simply and solely this; that it is good. Therefore, good simply and solely as such is the will's formal object. Now, good as such, is not finite, nor is it indefinite. It is infinite. But, again, as we have said, the formal object of a faculty is the measure of that faculty's capacity and potentiality. Hence, the capacity and potentiality of our being, the inward need and inmost want of our nature, the consequent and corresponding impulse of our will, and the essential movement of our love, these have an infinite object. Even were finite objects supposed to sufficiently explain the actual and definite acts of will that tend towards them; yet, no finite objects, however indefinitely numerous or great, could ever sufficiently explain the primal impulse and fundamental movement of our will, of which such acts are only subordinate results, secondary consequences, and surface tokens. Nay, the fact that will can love any good shows that its love can transcend any limits in good, and, therefore, shows that its love cannot be contented with any good that is not infinite. Therefore, our will's movement is towards an infinite object.

Well, you may say, all this only proves that, in the logical, ideal, abstract order, will has an infinite object.

Be it so, I may answer. This much at least I have gained, that, in the ideal order, we cannot sufficiently explain the movement of will without an object that is formally, although objectively, infinite. We have thus got so far as to lay down this assertion: The will is subjectively, that is to say, in its own actual being, a finite thing; but objectively, that is to say, in its potential capacity, it is a faculty tending towards an infinite object.

Now we advance into the region of reality, into the order of fact. Our will is a fact. Its movement is a downright fact. But movement cannot be towards nowhere. The movement of our will cannot be towards nothing. Its object must be a fact that is real, or a fact that can be actually rendered real. As, then, each particular act of will that is a fact, must have a real term in the order of facts, by the knowledge of which that real movement was aroused and in the real possession or actual realisation of which that real movement rests; so, the fundamental fact of impulse in our real nature, by which we are actually and essentially borne onward and outward with an infinite thirst of soul, with an infinite horizon of truth, with an infinite potentiality of love, this fact, this moving nature, this essential impulse, must have some sufficient explanation in fact. If you say that it is the nature of our Being, you say indeed what is a fact, but it is the very same fact that you have to account for. If you say you can't account for it, then say no more. If you say that there is, in the order of reality, a good that is infinite, and that our finite nature, being yet intellectual, is essentially made and fitted to seek that infinite good, and by clear knowledge and secure love to reach and hold it, and thus rest in a vitality of peaceful perfection, as well as in a happiness of contented love, then you have given a clear and real explanation of a clear and real fact. But an infinite good that is real, is God.

Repetition that would be useless and tiresome on trivial matters, is often a great help to understanding in matters which, from the depth of their meaning and the subtlety of their proof, involve finer abstraction, and consequently require more persistent as well as more careful use of thought. We may then set this same argument in another shape which will show it to some minds in a clearer light.

Human nature is a fact. It cannot, then, include within itself a positive contradiction; for, that would prove it to be an absurdity. Our nature is really and essentially impelled towards the real possession of a perfect good, and the consequent realisation of thorough happiness. If God exists, that natural movement of our nature has in Him an adequate object and proportioned term, and is capable therefore of reasonable explanation. If there be no God, there can be no such impulse, and therefore no such nature.

That there is such a fundamental impulse in our nature is not only evident from the limitless scope of our intellect which shows the way to our will, it is also plainly proven to experience by the reality of our desire for happiness and the reality of our boundless aspirations. We do not say that men are always, or even often, making actual acts of desire, actual longings, actual formal wishes of the kind. But, we do say that there is no one without a real soul-thirst, a real hunger of the heart, a real yearning and want within his inmost nature that can, does, and must love, and seek higher, nobler, truer good than such things as are passing and perishable, hollow, and exhaustible. We do say that such a real stretching forward and soaring upward of a nature cannot be stayed nor satisfied by what is immeasurably unworthy of itself, with what is bounded in perfection and shortcoming in attractiveness, with what it cannot reasonably give its boundless love to, with what it cannot, reasonably or unreasonably, regard as the real object of its deepest longings, or as the real crown of all its highest needs. We do say that by how much we are better than the brute, by so much are the wants of our nature nobler than can be glutted with matter. We do say that we have a boundless love that is real.

Now, if there be no reality corresponding to that real need of our nature, if there be no object proportioned to that real potentiality of our soul, then, is that capacity a myth that is meaningless; then, is that need a fancy that is vain; then, is that nature a phantom that is false. For, if there be no object, the fundamental need of our nature is a positive real want of what is really nothing. A nature with such a want is an absurdity; therefore, an impossibility.

Again, if there is a real and inevitable longing for something more than a finite object, there is a real need of it within our very nature. If so, such an object really exists. But, if there is no real infinite object, we have no real need of it. If we have no real need of it, we have no real capacity for it. If we have no real capacity for an infinite object, all our faculties can receive their complete perfection and thorough contentment from a finite object. If so, the objective range of all our faculties is finite. Yes, the objective range of all our faculties is essentially limited by fixed, definite conditions of time and space, of kind and of degree. If so, our faculties cannot rise above such conditions. If so, there is no such thing as abstract thought or immaterial aim. If so, intellectual action is only material perception, will is only material appetite. If so, it is absolutely impossible for me to write or for another to read this reasoning about abstract truths and immaterial worth. Thus, if you deny the real existence of God, you cannot admit any energy that is spiritual, any impulse that is noble. You will, then, turn towards matter to seek your animal paradise; and falling ever to lower depths, you will become more and more like the clay which you love, as you find a less and less satisfied, even though less and less remorseful delight, while you batten like a brute upon filth. Faugh! Materialist, how foul you are!

PROOF VIII

THE ACTUAL EXISTENCE OF POSITIVE AND DIFFERENT
DEGREES OF PERFECTION PROVES THE ACTUAL EXIST-
ENCE OF GOD

THIS proof is in itself very plain; although at first
sight it may not appear to be so, owing to the abstract
nature of some of the truths on which it rests. It is,
also, a very full proof, because it leads us to the knowledge of the Existence of God under the notion of All-
Perfect Being. It was one of the favourite proofs of
the old School-men. Now it is much less familiar,
because Philosophers, instead of leading the people up
to the understanding of most essential and therefore
most abstract principles, have pandered to the tastes
of the times, by stooping to make their lessons like
lectures of more concrete, and therefore less necessary,
science.

Perfection means completeness in good. This completeness may be only such as must be had, in which
case, it is relative perfection; or, it may be such as can
possibly be had, in which case it is absolute perfection.
Perfection may be said to be absolute when it includes
all possible good of a certain kind, or in one definite way;
but it is most properly called absolute, when there is an
utter absence of imperfection of any sort, and a thorough
possession of perfection in all good that is without flaw.

Quality is the tone or intensity of a perfection. We do sometimes talk of a bad quality; but then either we are speaking of what is morally wrong, though, in another way, good of its kind, or we are speaking of a real good in reference to the right perfection which it lacks, not in reference to the partial perfection which it owns.

When we give a reason for anything, this reason must be either one with the thing in question, or something else external to it. An intrinsic reason must in reality be identical with what it proves, although it may be distinct in thought. When the proof and the proven can be found, in fact, apart, when the existence of one does not logically include the existence of the other, the reason is not intrinsic but extrinsic or logically external. Thus, if I advance the nature of your Being as a reason for your unity, my reason is really identical, and therefore logically intrinsic. If I bring as proof of your physical existence, a reason drawn from your presence here in space, I am giving a reason that is not intrinsic to your own Being, since this can remain itself although transported otherwhere.

A result may be determined from within or from without. It may be a consequence wound up with the own nature of a thing, or it may follow from the action of something else. Being and energy, nature and action, are twin ideas under which are classed all that is or may be. Now, a real result, an actual determination, an existent state of things, is something. It is, then, either to be explained by Being or by Energy, by its own nature or by the action of another. But a result to be explained by its own nature, is a determination from within; a result to be explained by another's action is a determination from without. We call the first a *formal* determination, because it is so formally of itself. We call the second *effective* determination, because it is so effectively through another.

With regard to the way in which a perfection can be possessed; it may be had in its own direct kind; we then say that it is formally present, because it is there in its own form. It may, again, exist, not in its own definite sort, but in a higher manner which includes and adds to all its perfection, but excludes the imperfections that cling to it. For example, the authority of a policeman is formally present in Z. 999. It is eminently present in the Supreme power. Again, the power of painting is formally in the brush; it is eminently in the Artist. This eminent owning of perfection means, therefore, simply, the owning of it in a higher way. This higher way may, of course, be only comparative. The truest sense of eminent ownership is the superlative possession of perfection and the superlative absence of any and all imperfection.

As some modern critics either ignore this proof, or treat it with scant courtesy, I give some references to works of great Philosophers whom serious students may consult. St. Thomas of Aquin. (Sum. Theol. 1. p. q. 2. a. 3. Cont. Gent. B. 2. C. 15. De. Potent. q. 3. a. 5.) (St. Augustine De Trinitate B. 8. C. 3. De Civ. Dei B. 8. C. 6.) (Urrabura t. 1. p. 102.) (Schiffini p. 24 n. 391.) (Farges Idée de Dieu. pp. 118-125.) (Saisset Phil. relig. t. 2. p. 214.) (Hontheima. Theod. p. 141.) I quote the form under which this proof is put by the great German Jesuit Fr. Kleutgen, which is practically the same as that used by St. Thomas: "We remark in nature things more or less good, more or less true, more or less noble. Now, 'more' or 'less' are asserted of different objects according as they approach the different degrees of what is highest in the scale. There is then a being which is the true the good and the noble par excellence, and further this being, possessing in an eminent degree goodness, truth, and in consequence 'being,' must be the cause of any being goodness, perfection in all things. Now, the being which is the cause of that possessed by all things, we call God." (Kleutgen La Philosophie Scolastique t. IV. p. 294 Paris 1870). Fr. C. Delmas, S.J., one time Professor of Philosophy in the Jesuit Seminary at Vals, Haute Loire, sets the argument in this shape: "Things which possess a diminished degree of perfection in the line of 'being,' 'good,' etc., hold such perfection in participation from some other, which is in the highest degree Being, Good, etc. But there exist things which possess a diminished degree of perfection. Therefore there exists a Being which possesses all perfection. The proof of the first assertion is: That which has any perfection on its own account, i.e., of itself, does not possess it in a diminished degree; for no perfection of itself requires diminution; — e.g. Being Itself (Ipsum Esse) does not of itself lack *being;* nay more, supposing that quantity itself, be of itself actually existing, it would be infinite. If therefore we have less being, less good, etc., a thing endowed with these qualities cannot have 'being,' 'good,' etc., on its own account, i.e., of itself, it derives them from another. But there is not a 'processus infinitus' of beings deriving their perfection from another. Therefore there exists a Being which is of itself and from itself Being, not deriving anything from any other being."

First form of the proof: The reason for the positive possession of such and such degrees of perfection.

Take any definite existent quality. There must be a

reason for the particular degree of perfection in which it
is possessed. What is that reason? It must be either
an intrinsic or an extrinsic reason. Now, it is not an
intrinsic reason. Were it intrinsic, it should be either
drawn from the nature of the quality itself, or from the
nature of the individual being that actually owns it.
Neither of these can adequately or ultimately explain
why that quality is in such a degree and none other.
Firstly, the nature of the quality itself is no such sufficient explanation; because as a matter of fact, that
quality exists in lesser and greater degrees, so that its
nature cannot finally account, of itself, for the fact of its
being in one particular degree rather than in any other.
Secondly, the nature of the individual being, in which
that quality is realised, is no sufficient reason for the
definite degree of that quality. Think quietly and deeply
over the proof of this. If the individual nature of the
being were the sufficient explanation of the degree of its
quality, it would be so formally, that is to say, it would
be the formal and intrinsic reason for it. This would
mean that the reason for the individuality and the reason
for the quality of that being are formally the same.
This would mean that they are logically identical. This
would mean that these two notions, the actual individuality of that particular Being, and the actual kind of that
particular quality, cannot be realised apart, but as they
are logically identical, so are they, in fact, the self-same
thing. Hence, it would follow, that whenever that
particular kind of quality exists, it is identical with the
particular individual being in question. Thus, that
degree in perfection would be no more possible to be
realised except in that particular individual, than could
that particular individual exist distinct and apart from

itself. To sum up, briefly: The individual nature of the Being cannot be the logical and sufficient explanation of the degree or kind of its quality, because that would suppose this individuality and this degree in quality, to be not only in fact united, but in logical thought identical. Wherefore the sufficient explanation of degree in quality is not formally intrinsic. Therefore it is extrinsic. But, if such reason is extrinsic, the determination of that particular degree of quality is not formal but effective. In other words: whenever and wherever more or less is possible in perfection, then and there, the reason of the more or less actually realised, is not to be found in the intrinsic nature of the individuality of the Being, nor in the intrinsic nature of the quality possessed; but, it is to be sought for in extrinsic agencies, in a determination of fact caused from without.

Further, whatever is the full and determining cause of any quality or perfection must have the power of producing such a result. But, the power of producing a certain result must mean the possession of a perfection at least equal in degree, and, either formally like, or eminently including, the effect of which it is the cause. Otherwise, we should admit that what is nothing can do something. Again, this is true as long as there is question of degree in perfection. So long, the sufficient reason for it must be extrinsic. Thus, either we must admit that there is no ultimate sufficient reason at all, which is logical suicide; or we must admit that there actually exists a being in which the adequate reason for its perfection is intrinsic. Therefore, its individuality and its perfection are formally identical. Therefore, its concrete nature as a fact and its abstract nature as an essence are logically the same. Therefore, both are absolutely necessary. Therefore, it is its own determination in existence and in kind. Therefore, it is its own position in actuality, and its own affirmation of truth. Therefore, it actually is of itself, and its perfection is only bounded by impossibility. Therefore, it is essentially existent and absolutely perfect. But such a Being is God.

Again, in such a being we have the only full and final reason for the actual determination of more or less in perfection amongst Beings that have not an adequate intrinsic reason for themselves. But, such Beings as these actually do exist. Therefore, the being without the determination of which they could not exist, must be actually existent. Therefore God exists.

This argument may be applied to every positive notion that is realised. Thus, we can infer from the greater or lesser fullness of perfection in existence that the individuality of things which are not absolutely perfect is logically although not physically distinct from their existent perfection, and is not, therefore, intrinsic to the notion of what makes up their logical self. This proves that they are, as they are, owing to extrinsic determination, and, so, that there is a determining power outside them in which is realised the ultimate reason of perfection in existence. This ultimate reason must be the actuality of an existence which is logically identical with perfection, and, as all kinds and degrees lean upon it for their adequate "Why," it must be absolute in existence, and, in perfection, all-complete.

Second form of this proof: We must have some reason that will logically account for the negative exclusion of further degrees in existent and limited perfections. Why are there such and such definite limits in such and such definite Beings? They are not limited formally,

There is no reason intrinsic to the nature of the quality, nor is there any reason intrinsic to the nature of the individual, as such, that necessarily and of itself excludes a further and fuller degree. Therefore, the limitations which exist are effective. Therefore they are extrinsic. Therefore, the reason for them is to be found in some determining power from outside. This sequence must continue until we come to some Being which is its own intrinsic and sufficient reason for its own limitation. Such a Being must have all the perfection which is possible to it, because its own nature will only limit itself by excluding what is denied by its own position. Its only limit is its own nature, and its own nature has no limit within the circle of what is possible to it. Such a Being will exclude only what is impossible to it. But, as a being in which individuality and quality are logically intrinsic and identical, is simply its own existence, it can only exclude what is not compatible with the nature of own-existence. It can only, then, exclude what is impossible in itself, and what, to it, is impossible on account of imperfection mingled with it. In this way, we are brought to see that the ultimate reason for the existence of Beings that have a limit to their perfection, is the existence of a Being that has no limit to its perfection except limits set by the impossibility of its being, in any sense, imperfect. Thus, God is the ultimate explanation of sight, yet God can have no eyes, because while eyes are more or less perfect in their kind, their formal nature includes imperfection.

Do not condemn yourself by saying that the degree of perfection in anything is explained by the concrete existence of that particular Being, which, as a fact, is such and no other, so perfect and no more.

This would be a foolish roundabout way of saying: You want an ultimate reason for a fact. I will give it to you by supposing that it is given. I will explain this fact by stating that it is a fact. Do not say this. Say rather one of three things: that you deny what I say: but know nothing about it and wish to remain so; or, that a particular fact that is imperfect is an ultimate and sufficient reason for itself, a thorough and independent explanation of itself; or, that such a fact involves, for its ultimate and adequate explanation, the existence of a fact that is of itself absolutely perfect and ultimately self-sufficing. The last answer is the right one. The second answer asserts what is not self-existent and self-sufficing to be so. The first answer is an open and honest Confession of what in society, may be called Agnosticism, but which, at home, may be said to be the insolent dogmatism of affected ignorance. Work your brains a bit.

PROOF IX

LAW is a rule of reason. The word is, of course, used in many senses, as every other word may be. Thus, a constant and uniform mode of action is often called a law. We even find that, when "Exact Scientists" grow dizzy with the self-revolving consciousness of their success in one branch of practical knowledge, and fall into the conceit of supposing that they are prophets of all thought, and teachers of all men, they speak of law as though it were merely a name for a succession of similar phenomena.

As long as gentlemen, who are as dogmatic on their own side as they are sceptical towards others, wish to contribute fiction to magazines or enliven their lectures with fancy, no one should quarrel with their use of metaphor. But, in their turn, they must not ask us, even in the name of "Exact Science," to take their ignorance as a principle, or their metaphor as a proof. Certainly, we speak of the laws of bees and of ants, of the laws of gravitation and of motion, of the laws of affinities and of combinations. But, what men mean by these expressions is not the actual sequence of appearances under similar circumstances, nor the real sameness of result. This, men understand to be the following or observance of law, the keeping to a rule. What men mean by law is, properly, a rule that is followed. This meaning, we all know to be taken directly and primarily from rules laid down for the public and social guidance of men. It is necessary to be on our guard against some "Exact Scientists" who falsify words in order to slip in their own base metal under the stamp of human current coin. Any child could tell you that "The laws of the Country" is a plain phrase in plain English, and that when you speak of "The laws of ants" you are speaking of these interesting insects as if they were little people. Hence, it is both foolish and arrogant to try to warp this word so as to make it properly apply only to the facts themselves that occur in similarity of sequence. Even in this case, law must mean, in men's minds, an abstract rule in obedience to which these facts follow.

Wherefore, it seems an obvious expression of common sense, to say that law properly means, "A rule of reason." It means a direction given to action through thought and wish, through mind and will. Hence, law is said to bind because it is a definite determination coming from authority and rendering a definite conduct necessary. The word and notion of obligation come from this; for, by obligation we are obliged, that is to say, tied to a certain act or its omission. The obligation imposed by law may or may not be enforced by physical power. This is a consequence of law. It is not the obligation itself, but a material sanction justified only by the previous existence of obligation. Law and obligation are correlative. Law is the rule; obligation the ruling or application of that rule. Both involve the idea of necessity. Law, if true, includes essentially a "Must." Its obligation is none unless inevitable. Obligation holds the mind by means of a reasonable knowledge, and it holds the will by means of moral compulsion.

What is the explanation of the binding power of law? It means a necessity because it is not merely permissive but imperative. It does not mean a physical necessity such as forces us altogether independently of our own will, because law acts through mind and will. It means a real necessity, because we cannot free ourselves from it by merely wishing to do so. I must, of necessity, do what is a necessary means for the gaining of an end that I really wish to gain. But, if it is my own free choice that decides on my wishing to gain that end, my wishing to take that means to it, is only necessary dependently on my own wish. Such a necessity as this is not really a necessity at all, because it is only the result of my own wish. It is, then, free to me to take or leave it. It is, then, no necessity. The binding power of law means much more than this. It is not the result of the wish of those who are bound. It determines, it necessitates their wish, and, in this way, necessitates their action.

The binding power of law is, therefore, a real moral necessity. Now, a necessity that is real, and yet not physical, but moral, can be only conceived in this way. Beings that are unintellectual, or Beings that are intellectual when they are not determined formally, in as much as they are intellectual, may be acted upon by what we call blind or brute force. Intellectual beings, as such, act only, when an end having been presented by thought as attainable, their will wishes to attain it and, if needs be, sets their physical powers in pursuit of it. Now, if the choice or rejection of the end in question is quite in the power of the will, the will remains free. If, however, the object is such as the will cannot but wish, there is no freedom in its choice. The binding power of law is in its actually connecting a certain course of action with the attainment of an end which the will cannot but wish to attain. Of course, physical liberty is left, as long as a definite action is not with evident and absolute necessity seen to be evidently and absolutely necessary for the attainment of an end that is evidently essential and supreme. But, there is no moral liberty left, whenever an action is known, if not evidently and intuitively, at least by reasonable abstract certainty, to be bound up with the attainment of a supreme aim and end. In our actual kind of existence, our thoughts on such things are only abstract. Hence our physical liberty is only restrained by physical force. No moral force can physically constrain it. But, our moral freedom is limited by moral force. Moral force is the moral necessity of action consequent on the necessity of an end to be secured. This moral necessity is a binding of will through knowledge. The binding of will through knowledge is an obligation. Obligation is a result of law. Law is a rule of reason. It regulates action both because it acts on reasonable will, but most particularly and primarily because it comes from a rational principle, a power that can determine the means by which reasonable will can reach its end. Such principle and power must evidently be itself intellectual, and its action must be, in the most formal sense, intellectual.

Conscience may, in one sense, be said to be the internal principle of consciousness, or that by which we know what is passing within ourselves. This is a psychological sense. Conscience has also a moral sense. In this, it means our definite practical judgment as to what is right or wrong. We need not defend this use of the word. It is common and familiar amongst reasonable men. It is the sense in which we now speak of Conscience.

We have at last come to our proof. We ground it on a fact which no ignorance can doubt, and which no arrogance can deny. It is a fact that men distinguish between right and wrong. Let us turn over this fact well so as to master its full meaning.

First of all, the bare fact is this: All men hold firmly and with full conviction that certain things are wrong and to be of all necessity avoided, and that certain other things are of necessity to be done; that this distinction between right and wrong is essential; that this necessity of avoiding what is wrong, and of doing, at the right time and in the right manner and under the right circumstances, what is right, comes not from man's free will or choice, nor from any merely external or accidental consideration, but immediately and formally from the very inmost nature of things.

What is the bearing of this fact? We do not ask, how do men explain their belief in it; nor what proofs they give for their conviction of its logical necessity and of its reasonable grounds. Such a question as this might suppose that men should admit no principle that they cannot perfectly prove, and that they should follow no practice, the moral foundation and final reason of which they cannot clearly explain. This would be absurdly contrary to common-sense. It would mean that no man can have a direct and practical certainty without reflex and abstract science; that, forsooth, a man cannot have any reasonable knowledge unless he is a finished philosopher. No! The most evident truths and the most palpable facts are precisely those about which most men have the greatest and most reasonable certainty, and about which few men can talk scientifically without becoming incoherent, unsatisfactory and uncertain. What we do ask is this: Given this fact, are there not some evident conditions involved in it, from which we can, and must logically, draw conclusions, that are really, although only implicitly, in all men's minds; conclusions, which, when explicitly explained, most men will honestly recognise?

What is in men's minds when they all agree that a certain thing is downright wrong? Do they think it is a result of their own choice? Certainly not. They hold undoubtedly that the difference is not made by themselves, but is constituted, independently of their will, by an order inherent in the nature of things. Do they admit it to be a mere matter of taste, in the way in which one girl loves music, while another doats on sweets, or in the way in which "What is one man's food is another man's poison?" No. We know that the same inflexible rule of right and wrong is set for all. Can the difference which rational beings recognise between good and evil be accounted for by the becomingness existing in the nature of things? This is an aesthetic solution. It is true, as far as it goes, because moral good is becoming to a rational nature, moral evil unbecoming. But, it is false, if it is exclusive. If it denies any further rule of right and wrong, it is absurd, because it does not explain the one thing to be explained, namely, the moral "Must." In this theory, there would be no essential difference in kind, only a difference in degree, between a girl's untidiness in dress and her neglect of honour, between a man's bad management of his moustache and his committing murder. Both are unbecoming, one more so, the other less. Why do men look on one as a circumstance that is morally indifferent, and on the other as a crime to be morally condemned? Putting out of sight the consequences to others, do men still see a difference that is thorough and essential, within the very nature of things, between the two? Decidedly. One proof of it is in the praise or blame which they bestow. We admire beauty, or talent, or strength. We applaud taste, refinement, and dexterity. But we look on them as gifts, given or acquired, that throw no moral halo round the owner. We honour virtue as own worth. We consider the fulfilment of duty as the first, the highest, and the last necessity of life. We recognise that while in many things man may act as he lists, in some things he is bound by a stern moral "Must," and that, in these things, not in those, the nobility or degradation of a life consists. Were there no ultimate and essential reason in things for the "Must" which binds men to right, and restrains them from wrong, praise such as we give to virtue would be irrational, and punishment decreed against crime, a tyranny. Therefore is it that Nihilists and Communists grow powerful amongst the people where the prophets of Atheism have preached. The latter enunciate principles, and the former draw from them, with the evidence of logic, conclusions that are irrational in speech and, in use, fiendish. If there be no radical law, promulgated by reason itself, and binding man's will, with moral yet inevitable necessity, to act accordingly to its decrees, then, the "Great unwashed" cannot without tyrannical injustice be coerced into respecting what is becoming in conduct; then, the ruffian rabble bred in human hells, is quite right in appropriating the contents of your pocket, or even, if it amuses them, in taking your life. Why not? You can appeal to no principle that condemns their course, if you allow the foundation of morality to fall. If there is no "Must" in moral matters, there can be no real right. If there is no real right, life is left to the bitter ruling of brute force.

If there is a "Must" in moral matters, it means much more than "Ought," for this is only Counsel, the other command, this only exhorts, the other insists; this only shows what is becoming and beautiful, the other declares what is bounden and right; the one appeals to our sense of fitness, harmony, and order, the other addresses itself to our knowledge of duty, necessity, and law.

Do you admit this? Whether you do or not, makes the most absolute difference to yourself; to mankind it makes none. Your denial of it would set you on the side of a most insignificant, though noisy, most disreputable, though pretentious minority. Who do admit this? Speaking roundly, all men who have the use of reason hold to the principle. Speaking strictly, all men who are good, make it the main-spring of their lives. The almost complete universality of men who say that there is a strict and stringent moral "Must," cannot by you be put down as fools who know not what they say, nor as liars who conceal their real thought. Neither can the plain sense of what they say be twisted by intellectual sharpers into an underhand and illogical attempt to make the mere usefulness of morality, or its happiness, the full and final criterion of its own worth. That is not what sensible and good men think or say. They are convinced that good is the measure of use, not use the measure of good. They are convinced that happiness is the result, not the cause, the reward, not the rule, the consequence, not the measure, of right.

Will you say, as Utilitarians often do, that use is the rule of good, and good the rule of use? You shrink from so bare a contradiction. Which then rules the other?

Will you say that use is the rule of good? Then, usefulness is the first and final rule. Then, there is no rule above usefulness. Then, there is nothing for usefulness to be of use to. Then, usefulness cannot be useful to anything else, neither can it be useful to itself. Then, this opinion is silly.

Will you say, that good is the rule of use? What do you mean by good? There are only three kinds of good possible, the useful, the pleasant, the becoming. You cannot mean useful good, for that is only good because of something else. Do you mean good, in the sense of pleasure or happiness? In this sense, good is not the supreme rule of right. Firstly, because men all agree in deciding what is right or wrong on its own moral merits, independently altogether of its pleasurableness, immediate or remote. When they speak of happiness in reference to right, it is either as an incentive to action, not as a standard of judgment; or it is as an ulterior consequence of the true rule of right, not as an application of an intrinsic constituent of right. What in the long run is happy, is right. Does this prove that right is regulated by happiness? No. Men mean by it that true happiness is bound up with right; which is evidently and essentially true. What does it prove? It proves that right is not only the rule of use, but also the road to happiness. Secondly, pleasure and happiness need a standard whereby to judge whether they be right or wrong. There are pleasures that are foul, and there are pleasures that are noble. How do you discriminate between them? By their greater or lesser pleasure?

Good men do not answer so. By the kind of their pleasure? How do you decide upon the nobler kind? By the order to which it belongs? See! You are adopting another rule of right. Thirdly, is one's own pleasure, one's own first and highest rule of right; or is it the greatest sum of happiness for all? In the first case, you make each man to look on himself, an imperfect and insignificant item, as the final end and aim of the universe. In the second case, you make men to be only a means for pleasure. In both cases you destroy the rule of right. For, in the first case, you make this rule subjective, and dependent on one's own will. In the second case, you make this rule objective, in an ideal that is utterly unknowable in definite thought, and therefore practically, a mere "Will-o-the-wisp."

Will you say that good is the rule of use and the standard of conduct in this sense, that men should act in a way evidently shewn by reason to be suitable to their nature? We are again back at the fitness of what is right following on the becomingness of things. The nature and order of things, which, of itself, renders one's moral action a right and harmonious exercise of reason and of will, does decide, oftentimes and directly, between what is right and what is wrong. But, again and again, by the law of conscience men understand much more. It is a law, law means "Must." "Must" means, in rational life, a moral necessity. Moral necessity means a necessity arising from an end and aim that is of necessity to be attained. Such a supreme end and aim of human life does, then, exist; for, the law of which it is the source, exists. Now, a supreme end and aim of human life that is a fact in the actuality of its influence, and a principle of the moral necessity of law, cannot but have a sufficient reason for itself both in the physical and in the intellectual order of things. Such sufficient reason must be, at the same time, a fact, and a first source of necessary truth. But a fact that is a first source of necessary truth is a fact that is itself both necessary and intellectual. But a fact that is both necessary and intellectual is a self-existent personal Being; and a self-existent personal Being is God. Wherefore, God exists.

This reasoning is much more diffuse than that usually followed by thinking men. They say: There is a law of conscience; for, we know that we must avoid evil and do good. Therefore, there is a real moral necessity ruling human conduct. Therefore, there is a supreme aim and end of human life, and a Supreme Ruler. Both are God.

In other words: Our conscience tells us that we must avoid certain things that are wrong, and do certain things that are obligatory. Therefore, there is a moral necessity. Therefore, there is a moral law. Therefore, there is a foundation and a source of moral law. Therefore, there is a moral end and a Moral Ruler of the world, Therefore, there is an absolute truth, a supreme good, a perfect worth, a primal right. This is the First Lord and Final Judge of all. This is God.

PROOF X

THE ORDER EXISTING IN THE UNIVERSE PROVES THE EXISTENCE OF GOD

REVIEWS owe whatever healthy life they have to the crumbs that are thrown to them from the minds of great men, but their daily bread is either the dough of over-hurried cleverness or the sodden stuff of unconscious mediocrity. Fledglings of a militant and noisy kind flap themselves into states of enthusiastic and defiant self-assertion. Dunces of the flabby and lazy type settle down into dogmatic denials of whatever would ruffle their comfortable ignorance.

A few years ago, there was a great cackling and crowing in English Reviews about the "Argument from Order." Very few of the writers had any other qualification for speaking than their own eagerness to be heard. Some few could write pleasant nothings about anything, everything, or nothing. Some other few had credentials which entitled them to speak with authority on totally different subjects. Few of them had had any real philosophic training. They were all on the same side, in their little corner of the intellectual world. The young cocks strutted and crowed. The fat geese cackled and blinked. There was a tremendous chorus. "The argument of Order must now be finally abandoned," vociferated the young ones; while the heavy birds "Failed to see it."

Now, it so happens that this is a matter which belongs directly and immediately to the domain of human reason. It does not depend on the electric light nor on the perfection of sewing machines. Science, as it is called, that is to say, the least of all sciences, that one, namely, which treats of the most material qualities of things, is no help towards the solution. A betting-man is as good an authority about it, as a lecturer on Chemistry. A mathematician is here on a level with a cabman or a milk-maid. It is nothing more and nothing less than this: does a certain conclusion follow logically from a certain evident and undeniable state of facts. There can be no question about the facts; so fact-sciences have nothing to say to it. It is purely a question of pure reason. Philosophy properly so called, "the Science of the ultimate reasons of things," is sole judge of this. But, just as all young ladies enunciate decisions on music, so, all review-writers feel called upon to be the spokesmen of intellectual thought.

That the argument from order has something in it, and is not to be contemptuously thrust out of court, is plain to the unprejudiced from the way in which it is accepted by many and wise men. It is frequently to be found in those Books which by multitudes of all peoples, amongst them the loftiest minds and the noblest characters of the world, are held sacred as the very Word of God. Thus, it is set forth with magnificent emphasis in the closing chapters of the Book of Job. Again, this argument seems to be the very first to catch the thought and touch the heart of those who most love nature, and most easily learn from her, so that the child, the savage, the poet, and the philosopher, beholding the marvellous order of the universe, bow down at once in spirit before the mysterious presence of an Ordainer. They may not all be able to unravel all the web of argument which unconsciously they have woven; nor, as is the case with every important human conclusion, can they dissect the living knowledge which they know they have. But they honestly believe that they see an order pervading nature; that this order is not absolutely rooted in nothing; nor the outcome of only such energies as are not self-sufficing; but that it comes from and depends upon some real First Principle of Order.

Against these, what do little reviewers in this little span of months, in this little space of England, say? They say, that there is no need for the "Interference" of an external agent to keep the universe in order. They say, that the order which exists in the world is simply the natural outcome which must result from the natural working of the nature of things. They say, that nature is the sufficient source of energies which inevitably harmonise in an equilibrium of order. Those of them who are reckless enough to plunge into the depths of rational explanation, have at first a great deal of practical and interesting information to give about material facts which have come to their knowledge, and which have nothing to do with the question. But, then, their foolhardy wits carry them out of their own safe and shallow sciences. They talk pretty things about a lady called "Nature," or write queer poetry about an unscientific ancestor of the future, known to them as their "Fatherman." After this they become incoherent, hysterical, and finally collapse into some such wild statement as this: "Nature is a realm governed by uniform laws, and based upon impenetrable darkness and eternal silence." (Huxley. "Life of Hume," page 44.) I have had a great, deal to do with boys of many nationalities and of every shade of stupidity, yet amongst all the absurdities of answers given to simple questions, I have never met anything so utterly silly or so conceitedly insolent as this: that two nothings, darkness and silence, the one impenetrable and the other eternal, are nevertheless sufficiently solid to support a whole realm of reality which is moreover governed by uniform laws!

When sifted and simplified the answer of many Atheists comes to this: The order existing in the Universe does not prove the Existence of God, because we suppose this order to exist without God. As they start from the assumption of what is really at issue, they are all through "Begging the question." Other Atheists doggedly deny that there is any reason for the fact. This means that there can be a fact without a reason for it. Other Atheists, again, hold that nobody can know anything about it; which assertion would be less conceited and more common-sense were they to limit it to the mere mentioning of their own mental incapacity or wilful blindness. Finally, and this is the class comprising all Atheists who are neither blind nor bad, some men really think that nature itself is sole and sufficient explanation of the order which exists in the world. For this last class alone we write, and we are thoroughly convinced that, if they quietly and dispassionately examine their own ideas, they will find there the very thoughts which we now suggest. First, we wish to warn them against undertaking too much. We want to prove very little at present; only this: That there is a First Principle of Order, Who, whatever else may or may not be said of Him, is an Intellectual Being.

That, in the world, there is a real order, which if not

perfect, is yet very complex and complete, we need not stop to show. The fact is ever and unmistakably before us. Now, we take a step further. This order must have some rational explanation, which is, for reason, final; and in fact, sufficient. Such explanation must be grounded either on the nature of things themselves, or on the existence of a power beyond and above the things that make up the ordered world. But, the nature of these things is not itself adequate to fully account for the order which is realised in and by them. Take care, at this point, not to presuppose what must be proved. Do not say: The Universe is made up of many and various elements, working according to uniform and necessary laws. These elements are simple and real facts. These laws are mathematical necessities. This much given, and it is undeniable, order must essentially result, and there is no need for any *Deus ex machina*. Quite so; but you are stealing your principles of proof. It is exactly what you take for granted, that is in question. The fact which you assert is undeniable; but you offer no explanation of the fact. How do you account for the ordered co-existence and ordered co-operation of these elements? What is the first and final basis of order in your elemental facts and uniform figures? Do not explain order by supposing its principles to be given. This order is a fact. Thus far, we are at one. Here is the issue: Is this order thoroughly and ultimately self-explanatory; or, being insufficient of itself, does it postulate, and, therefore, prove the existence of an independent and self-sufficing First Principle of Order?

We may distinguish two kinds of order. One we will call the order of harmony, the other the order of melody. The first is the co-existence in time and space of things so fitted to combine that not only are they a mutual help, but, without such union, many of them, at least, would be quite useless. The second is the successive unfolding or working of things so as to attain some object, reach some term, or fashion some effect. The first is more directly concerned with being or nature. The second is more immediately referred to action or energy. In both there is "The direction of means towards an end," which we understand to be a fair definition of order.

With regard to the first kind of order, there can be no question of its reality in the world. The multitudes of species and the variety of kinds that are given, are so fitly selected, so accurately placed, and so timely chosen that they do not form a chaos, but an admirably ordered universe. There would be less wonder, were some great power to actually intervene with guiding stroke or ruling measure in the harmony of the spheres. There is more wonder, in that the teeming usefulness of co-ordinate kinds by their clash and strife as well as by their help and service, are and act so as to be one. It is, indeed, open to any clever man, to deny plain facts in the way which pleases him most. In the extreme of Idealism, a German dreamer may say that all things are merely logical limitations of one Absolute. In the extreme of Materialism a British experimentalist may assert that everything comes out of an omnipotent protoplasm. Yet, men or women of the world who apply their common-sense even to these matters, don't take such opinions very seriously. We deliberately take it for granted that a cow and the grass which it is to feed on, are really different things. Now, how comes it to pass that there is beef for men, grass for cows, and elements for vegetation? As a fact, we have them all in the world; but

how are we to account for the ordered co-existence of all?
Even if the nature of the cow were sufficient explanation
for its own essence and existence, it cannot sufficiently
account for the grass. Without grass, the cow cannot
get on, but the cow cannot create grass, nor can the fact
of the grass necessitate the realisation of the cow. Thus,
in every way, in every kind, we have a most necessary,
a most subtle, and almost unending inter-dependence of
things that suppose but cannot produce each other.
You cannot reasonably say that the fact of the universe
accounts for the whole, just as each individual member,
or part, or atom accounts for itself. No. There is no
reality in the whole beyond the realities of all the parts.
Let each part be its own justification. You have still
to explain how they are all not merely realities, but
parts; not merely existing but existing in such definite
kind, number, degree, time, space, as to make up the
order of the universe.

Surely, it cannot be chance that is the cause of order.
That would be an amusing remark if made by a German
philosopher, because we know that they make serious
jokes about the identity of Nothing. But, in English,
chance means a relative absence of order.

Shall we, then, say that because each piece of metal
which goes towards making up a machine, is simply a
bit of substance, given us by nature, so, the machine can
be accounted for without the intervention of mind?

What are we to say about this big machine of the
world? Once the parts are together, it works naturally.
It does not require to be wound up; and it can keep
itself in repair. That makes it all the more wonderful.
If a machine is a proof of an intelligent direction of
means towards an end, it would seem plain that a result

which requires an immeasurably more accurate choice, and an inconceivably more subtle adaption of means towards an end, should show intellect. To give all the credit to natural forces governed by uniform laws, is only putting the question back.

Do not draw a woeful face, mumbling weird words about "Eternal Silence" and "impenetrable gloom." Do not wave your wizard wand, chanting fairy formulas about "protoplasms," "origin of species," "altruism," "your Father-man," or "the greatest sum of happiness," until with wild crescendo you burst out into the pet chorus of the pantomine: "Evolution."

In this age of ours, which is so admirable in most material ways, so petulant in many matters of thought, which sets itself with such manly thoroughness to sift the secrets of Nature, and which yet, with such phenomenal foolishness, ignores the knowledge winnowed by the thinkers of old, men may chance to pick up some grain of truth, and glory in their treasure-trove as though it were not the actual property of someone else. Perhaps in some future time, a clever engineer may believe himself to be the first inventor of the steam-engine, just as in our days a clever logician, Sir William Hamilton, was unaware that Aristotle knew more about the "Quantification of the Predicate" than he did himself. Or, perhaps, some genius may yet discover that two and two make four. Thus, Monism is only an old Pantheism under a new label. A new name does not always create a new thing. Evolution? It is an old story told by old men long, long ago.

Fourteen centuries ago, all the principles of Evolution that are not irrational were taught by the great Augustin. He held that all things at first existed only as *Semina*

rerum, that there was at first in things only the potency
of what, under the action and reaction of strong or slow
forces, they should become; that during days which
were epochs of unmeasured duration and of cumulative
result, the Moulder of the world worked merely through
natural elements and uniform laws, until the universe
crystallized into order. He held indeed, as all who are
not Materialists must hold, that man's spiritual soul was
not made of mere mud nor begotten of a monkey, but
was created by the immediate power of God. Since
Augustin, this theory has been commonly accepted as a
probable hypothesis by Christian Theologians.

There is as much wonder in an acorn as in an oak. In
that bewildering world of interlocked atoms or rebound-
ing vortices, of subtle gas or seething vapour, of dizzy
whirl or aeonic change, of molten mass or adamantine
ice, of eddying unison, or of titanic clash, there was the
potency, the germ of all that is or shall be.

Now we look upon the branching forth of that strange
power, which then was in the seed. But to go no further
than an acorn for ultimate explanation of an oak, is to
stop short upon the threshold of thought. To account
for the oak, the acorn, and the universe, by the virtue of
some primitive cell which held within itself the potency
of all worth and the energy of all power, which, yet, had
no cause, no reason other than itself, is to change science
into superstition, and to learn history from the "Arabian
Nights."

The question is the same whether we ask for an ultimate explanation of the germ or of its development, of
the seed or of its fruit, of the potency of a protoplasm or
of the perfection of the Universe. Order needs to be
explained whether it be considered in its folded bud or

open flower, in its dying seed or growing stem, in its
first impetus and aim or in its final halt and term, in its
mature world as we see it, or in its infant stage of simple
elements and uniform laws.

What about these natural forces and uniform laws?
The natural forces are so chosen and combined as to
result in a harmony which must not be set down to chance
nor to nothing.   These uniform laws are merely abstract
expressions of an acting Principle of Order.   This acting
Principle of Order is real.   Otherwise it could have no
real result.   It must have within itself, or it must lean
upon, some real necessity that is independent and
absolute.   This real necessity must be a First Principle
of Order, such as indefinitely surpasses in range of action
and in sublimity of kind, all order which we regard as
proof enough of intellectual energy.   Now, a reality and
a necessity like this, must be intellectual; because it is
far more than a mere source of measureless action; it is
a Being which has conceived the laws in obedience to
which nature works out order.

Laws, as they are realised in fact, are the actual submission to necessary rules of action.   These necessary
rules of action are logically pre-supposed to the submission yielded to them.   In their abstract character
they are intellectual necessities, but not facts.   Now,
intellectual necessities that are not facts, must have a
foundation in real fact.   They cannot be logically
founded on real facts which logically presuppose them;
for that would make a very "Vicious Circle."   On the
other hand, the order of real facts, logically presupposes
intellectual necessities of order.   Thus, realised order
logically presupposes uniform laws or ideal order, and
uniform laws or ideal order logically presuppose a real

fact-foundation. We are forced back logically from the real to the ideal; then, from the ideal to the real. If we take these two dependent orders to logically bolster up one another, we are putting our neck into a logical noose. What way is there out of it? There are two ways. One is, to admit that we don't understand it, and that it would be very impertinent of us to read lectures to those who do. The other way is, to open our eyes and see just this much. There is no logical possibility of explaining the order of the world, unless there be a First Principle of Order, real and intellectual, in whom the two orders of truth and of fact are physically and logically identical, in whom the most absolute necessity and the most supreme independence are essentially and infinitely self-own, from whose immutable truth all law and logic are derived, by whose Omnipotent Will all fact and reality exist.

If such a Being exists, the order of the world is capable of rational explanation.

If such a Being do not exist, it logically follows that there is neither truth nor fact. But, what is more immediately to our purpose, if such a Being do not exist, we must admit to the bitter letter, that "The realm of reality, governed by uniform laws, is based upon impenetrable darkness and eternal silence." What a pity that the Prophets of darkness cannot sit down and keep quiet on a basis of silence!

With regard to the second kind of order, that which we have taken the liberty to call the order of melody, it consists in the order inherent in nature, by which each thing in its own kind works out its own end. It may seem strange to some that we speak of this as order; for, many look on order as if it must always be accidental or on the

outside. No. We are speaking of an order that enters
into the essence of things, that reaches to their very
inmost kind, and is the inevitable unfolding of their very
own. Some Atheists fancy they have scored when they
get to the natural order, for then they can hide behind
"The nature of things." We are going to follow them
there.

First of all, the more intimate and essential the order,
the more thoroughly does it answer to the highest notion
of order. For, whatever may or may not be the explanation of it, an order that is implanted in being itself,
is much more than an order which merely varies in some
outside or accidental way, the nature of that being.

Now, everything in the world has the seal and necessity
of order stamped upon its essence. It must be, and it
must work according to its kind. That is a fact. All
science leans upon it. Now for the principle. What is
the logical explanation of this fact? Every fact is a
truth, and every truth that is not a first truth has its
proof and its full justification.

Is each and every nature a full and perfect logical
explanation of itself? No. Firstly, because there is no
self-sufficing reason within it for the fact of its own
existence, and until we get to some existence that is
self-sufficing we have no sufficient logical explanation
for the fact of any existence. Secondly, what we most
wish to insist on here, it has no self-sufficing reason within
it, for the order within its essence. Why? Because if
its own essence were self-sufficing, there would be no
impulse in it towards any further perfection. The final
order within created things is the consequence of their
incompleteness, and therefore the proof, that, whereas
they are not self-sufficing, so they cannot be self-existing.

In this order within essence, there is a realised truth which is proof of the reality of a necessary condition. In the real existence of anything upon earth, there is a real truth, dependent, subordinate, derived. Such truth, as it cannot ultimately explain itself, postulates the real existence of a First Principle, in the full infinity of Whose perfection are found the final reasons for the ideal fitness of things; for the practical reality of essence; for the final purpose that is, knowingly or not, worked out; for the direction within each nature of means towards an end; and thus, for the melody which in each thing, in its own tone, re-echoes something of the life of God.

PROOF XI

ERROR is an accident. It is always the result of causes that hamper or hinder the natural working of the mind. Thought, of itself, is true. As mind is a mirror, it must reproduce the likeness of what is set before it.

As mind is an immaterial mirror, it can have within itself no physical flaw, nor can the accuracy of its image be marred by any hitch in its gear or blemish in its surface. Mind is no mere machine. A material agent must, indeed, have material limits to its range, and material bars to its working. But, an intellectual agent is as universal in its vision, as truth is in its evidence. Mind is as knowledgeable as truth is knowable. Thus, the fact that it can mirror whatever is true, is proof that it will accurately mirror any truth that is properly set before it.

Mind only says what it sees; for, its sight and its speech are one. It only sees what is true; for, nothing but truth is its object. The taking of what mind says and sees as if this were a full account of reality is where error enters. Here a mistake may easily be made. Yet this can only happen when the image of reality, though true as far as it goes, does not go far enough to be a practical reproduction of fact. Even thus, error would be only remotely possible, were there not other influences which prevent the patient and broad gaze of thought, and which force the mind to look between narrow lines at truths that are chosen for a conclusion's sake. Mind is hurried along by will. What it sees at a glance is afterwards taken as a final and full decree; or thought is recorded for use, with hypothesis and limitation left out. The vision of the mind is perfect, but its use of sight may be easily interfered with.

> "For, all too late comes counsel to be heard."
> "When will doth mutiny with wit's regard."

But interference with its natural working is accidental to the nature of mind. Error, then, is an accident.

From this it follows that if we could show a particular conviction of a particular mind to have been arrived at without any influence of prejudice or of passion, we should have a sterling guarantee of its truth. To do this in individual cases is seldom easy. When done, it is seldom evident. There may be a lurking suspicion that some loophole has been left open, or there may remain that kind of misgiving which comes from inability to grasp at once all the threads of an argument. But, when we find a conviction practically as universal as reason itself, a conclusion identical in every possible phase and vicissitude of circumstance, a conclusion arrived at from the most opposite starting-points, held against the most hostile influences from without, and revered in spite of the most bewitching seductions from within, then, indeed, we know that it has been sifted from every possible chance of error, and that if we can know anything, we know its truth.

Now, this is the case with man's belief in God. The nature of God is a question that is abstract, intricate, and beyond the unaided powers of ordinary men to satisfactorily solve. Hence it has received the most varied and conflicting answers in men's minds. But, this wide divergence and common error as to the nature of God, throws a side light startling in its vividness, upon the one broad human agreement as to the evidence that there is a God. This latter statement regards a truth that is practical and primal, simple and tangible. It is a simple straight conclusion drawn almost intuitively by reason from simple and straight truths.

The human race believes in God. We must first establish this fact. It is to be proved as facts are proved by witnesses. In the first place, then, we appeal to the records of human life. All histories of all times, all peoples, and all places are full of this. They tell us of the religious rites and sacrifices, of sacred laws, of superstitious practices, of festivals, of reverence or of fear of some Divinity. Again, all travellers bring back the same tale, varied indeed by every shade of added doctrine, but in this one point identical, that all nations acknowledge the existence of some great Spirit, of some Power that is supreme.

Further, almost all the great thinkers of the world who expressly undertook to prove the truth of God's existence, have laid great stress upon this very conviction of mankind.

Now, great philosophers may fail in the cogency of their reasoning or fall into a conclusion that is false; but they are scarcely likely to base their proof upon a principle that is not sound. Nay, they set their arguments upon grounds which they understand to be admitted as solid even by their foes.

As a matter of fact, most modern Atheists find themselves forced to allow that there is a moral unanimity amongst men as to the existence of God. These gentlemen do not quarrel with this part of our proof. They throw us the fact, but they condescend to deny its meaning. They confess to a sort of serene pity for the ignorance and stupidity of the human race, and they generously offer to dispel the darkness of the world with the light of their own doubt or to deepen it with the shadow of their own dream. But, for the moment we are concerned only with the reality of the fact itself.

In the second place, the fact that all men do believe in God, is told in the material traces which this fact has marked upon the world. Listen to one who had learnt to put in worthy human speech, the worthiest ideas of human-hearted men. Cicero says: "This doth appear a most strong argument why we should hold that God exists: That never was there people so savage, none so brutal, as not to have a mind penetrated with the thought of God." The writings left by old ages, the poems of primitive peoples, the songs they sang, the stories which they handed down, the altars they set up, their statues, pictures, bricks or groves, their coins, their graves, the ornaments which their women wore, or the symbols of peaceful firesides and happy homes, their weapons of war, their harvestings, the detail of their life that touched their hearts most deeply or that toned their minds most thoroughly to thoughts of nobler things: these assuredly are tokens of the fact that they knew there is a God.

Now, come to the meaning of the fact, the force which it has to prove the truth of what it holds. The human race believes in God; therefore, God exists. We have to show the logical necessity of this sequence.

A constant and universal conviction must be taken to be a natural outcome of evidence acting on thought. It is, then, in lawful possession as a recognised and admitted principle. It has no need to prove its title or to make good its claim. Should doubt be cast upon its right, such doubt is to be considered groundless unless it can be proved. Peaceful ownership must reasonably be held to be legitimate, until the appeal that would oust it can be supported by solid argument. Much more, must those widespread and genuine judgments, which own a first place in the minds and lives of men, receive from us the reverence which is due to truth. To prove them to be false, it is not enough that eccentric wits should say they cannot see them, or that flippant scribblers should set them aside as the bogies of babies or the drivellings of priests. If learned lecturers who "wax fat and kick," scientists who make money by physical research and then get spasms of atheistic declamation, if gentlemen who are wise in chemistry and fools in metaphysics, at-home in the dissecting-room and bewildered in Theology, if they would only either "Stick to their last" or study what is above them, they would understand that if they will not be silent, they must try to prove what they say, for they attack a conviction more deeply and more securely rooted in men's minds than are the first principles of "Exact Science." The fact that men universally believe in God, is proof that God exists, unless it can be evidently shown that this conviction is not the natural outcome of thought but the result of accident.

Yet, we go further. We will take the possible sources of error, and show how the belief in God cannot have come from thence. You must, then, suppose some cause for this error which has thus led the mass of men astray; for, men do not err unless there be some positive cause to thrust their reason aside from its natural object, truth. But, as this supposed error is universal in time and space, you must find out for it a cause equally widespread and unfailing. Now, the mind cannot determine itself to form any definite judgment. It must be determined either by evident truth, or by the influence of will. In the present case, you do not admit that the mind is determined by evident truth. You must, then, hold that it is determined by will. Again, to explain the existence of this particular error, you must bring forward some motive sufficiently intense and extended, to invariably and ceaselessly move the human will so as to wrench the human mind into the unnatural assertion of falsehood. Yet, on the other hand, all the motives which we know by experience to incline the will towards wrong, and for its sake towards error, are all adverse to the belief in the existence of a God, not in favour of it. As a matter of fact, we know from the lives of most practical Atheists that both the pride and the passion of human nature are in revolt against the very notion of God; so that, in truth, the evidence for the existence of God must be so plain to men's reason as to conquer the opposing influences of will. In proportion as men are more noble in their thought and more worthy in their life, so do they recognise with greater clearness, and realise with greater reverence, the reality of God. As men are more material in their minds, and more earthly in their actions, so do they first fail in virtuous conduct, and then seek to hide their guilt with Atheism, or at least lessen it with doubt. This is a broad human rule grounded in all times and peoples on a knowledge of the world. To any human rule there are exceptions. It is a sort of necessity in moral things. But, that only makes the general law still more remarkable. Good men believe in God. Bad men rebel against the known truth, or lean towards Atheism. Belief in God is not due, therefore, to any evil influence of will.

Again, a conviction must be most deeply rooted in the evidence of truth itself, which has stood the test of every difficulty, which in the lapse of time is left still more secure, which is bound up with the highest culture of intellect and the most practical nobility of will, which has fearlessly fostered true science and unfailingly outlived the prophets of science that was false, which has been held by the human race to be an indispensable condition of human worth, and the absence of which has, by the moral unanimity of men, been always regarded as a consequence of pride or passion. Now, the conviction that there is a God, has been and is admitted, by the overwhelming majority of men, to be a conviction such as we have described.

Yet again, consider the obstacles which this conviction has always had to encounter, and you will see that, to have overcome them, it must be the decision of reason itself. The barbarity of many peoples, their vices, the catching sophisms of free-thought, and the alluring arguments of free-morals, the poisonous over-growth of polytheism and the sickening influence of superstition, the plausible or daring denials of fashionable Atheists and the uncouth or stupid dronings of dry-as-dust defenders: these are some few of the adversaries which this conviction has had to conquer. Yet, while against it was all that is seductive in pleasure and all that is high sounding in phrase, men have always clung to this

Conviction at the cost of sacrifice, with head and heart
and hand staking all their hopes in life and death upon
the fact of the existence of God. Bah! It is hard to
be patient with nonsense. Before assuming that
human reason has been in the wrong, might we not
suppose that it was right? All men know that there is
a God, and who or what are you?

One point well worth noticing here is that the notion
of the Godhead, instead of being gradually made more
clear as time went on and culture spread, was more and
more distorted, more and more wrapped up with superstitious follies, more and more warped so as almost to
become a mask for vice. This thoroughly upsets Atheistic fancies about the evolution of religion. Monothe-
ism came before Polytheism. Christianity changed
this, and being a new and full exposition of the first
Revelation, established the Unity of God for ever.
But, up to Christianity, men, as men must, aiding their
own reason with the teaching of the wise, did not look
forward towards lecturers or experimentalists, but
looked back towards a primal Revelation, for doctrines
of untainted truth. Thus, Diodorus Siculus says that
the old Chaldeans held a religion of pure tradition, and
did not, like the Greeks, seek to discover something novel
by the exercise of their own ingenuity. Plato tells of a
reproach addressed by the Egyptian Sages to the Greeks.
The Sages held that the true religion was the one handed
down from generation to generation, and they blamed
the Greeks for ignoring this. It is a rule of Aristotle,
often also insisted on by Plato, that to discover the
truth we must find out what was said of old, what was
the primitive doctrine, for this was the teaching of
God. It was the opinion of Socrates that our early

progenitors have transmitted to us sublime lessons taught originally from on high. There are many similar assertions to be met with in Cicero who constantly declares antiquity to be the best guide in religious belief. Lucan's line is well known, as an echo of a universal thought: *Dixitque semel nascentibus Auctor, Quidquid scire licet.* Again, the most excellent maxims of morality have been found not only amongst the Jews, but also amongst the Persians, Babylonians, Bactrians, Indians, Egyptians, Arabs, etc., who all concur in assigning the origin of these maxims to a primeval tradition, and in asserting that religious truth was first communicated to earth from Heaven. There must be some foundation for this. We do not here undertake to prove that there was a divine Revelation, but we bring forward the fact of there being a general and ancient belief in such a Revelation in order to offer an easy answer to Atheists who strangely seek to show, from the similarity of positive doctrines in all religions, that there is no real religion at all.

One word, now, with regard to the mental attitude taken by some few clever men in this matter. Tyndall says that the study of science tends to withdraw the mind from religion, or what he insolently calls superstition, "Not by reasoning, but by rendering the soil unfit for it." First of all, that must needs be a very narrow kind of study and it must needs be blinded by overweening vanity or savage bitterness, were it to render the mind unfit for receiving the seed of truth. Tyndall can scarcely mean as much as this. What he probably does mean is that the habit of dealing with sensible, tangible, physical proofs of fact renders the mind less liable to be impressed by proofs of a more abstract nature. This is true where there is exclusiveness. If a man only deals with one class of reasoning his powers are, of course, narrowed.

Contrast with this saying of Tyndall who is a clever experimentalist and a poetical writer, a saying of Lord Bacon who was, in every intellectual branch, a really great man. Bacon says that "Light sips of Philosophy may perchance incline the mind towards Atheism, but deep draughts bring it back to Religion."

PROOF XII

WITHOUT GOD THERE IS LEFT CHAOS

EVEN the most forward Agnostic will scarcely admit that there is in the world only the emptiness of nothing, and the utter absence of order. We may, then, begin to build on this ground that the Universe is not chaos. Now, we go on to say that truth of principle is realised in the existence of a fact. Physical reality is a positive assertion of every principle, whether absolute or relative, that is involved in itself or pre-required for its being. Hence, the actual existence of energy, of order, of knowledge, is not only a practical result, but also a logical affirmation of power, of principle, of truth. But, the truths enunciated in the existence of a fact, have a hierarchy of logical force which represents the degrees of essential necessity in which they are required for the physical reality of that fact. In other words, the place which principles or truths hold, with regard to one another, in the logical order, is not a mere subjective arrangement of ideas; it is the subjective rendering in thought of the objective truth in things.

Now, to deny an essential condition required for the very existence of an actual fact, would be to deny what is fundamental in that fact. It would be absurd to admit the existence of a fact, and yet deny its possibility. But, the world is admitted to be neither the vacancy of nothingness, nor the mere confusion of chaos. The world is, therefore, admitted to be an affirmation in fact of actuality and of order. But, again, this fact-affirmation involves, and logically rests upon, the affirmation of higher truths and deeper principles. First and foremost of all, it asserts the reality of what is most of all essential for its own possibility. This is God.

To stop short at the outside surface of things, to recognise with delighted triumph such physical results of facts as the lesser sciences can register for use, and yet to ignore with supercilious impatience such realised truths as are identical with the facts themselves, this is not rational. If there is any truth in Chemistry or Mechanics, much more is there truth in Mathematics, still more in Metaphysics; for, the truth of the former depends on the truth of these, not vice-versa. A fact is a fact through and through. A great deal of "modern Thought" is occupied with preaching up that side of facts which works on sight or smell or hearing, and with preaching down that side of facts which appeals to reason. But a fact cannot be thus split up. It stands or falls as it is. It is no fact, or it is all fact. Hence, that there is a realised reason in the fact of the world which must either give or get a logical explanation of itself, is an assertion that cannot be shaken by the brutal denial of a Positivist nor by an Agnostic's sentimental doubt.

Indeed very few Atheists fall so far foul of commonsense, as to refuse any answer to the world's "Why?" Those who do, we may safely leave behind us. They can do no good, and they can do no harm excepting to themselves. We openly assume that there is a reason realised in the world that gives the reason for it. Most Atheists are with us here. We take this ground, and we start to build on it. We will set our Atheists themselves

to work. Even though they call it "Impenetrable
gloom," or "The nature of things," or "The Unknowable," they admit that they can lay a solid grip on the
absolute and inevitable need for some sort of necessity.
In the physical order they have "Uniform laws." They
have, then, actual, existing forces which work harmoni-
ously and ceaselessly in utter obedience to abstract rules.
As far as physical science goes, it emphatically teaches
that there is a physical necessity in these forces or in
these laws. It does not say whether there be an absolute
logical need of affirming such necessity. Physical
science rests on the fact of physical necessity in things.
It has no business with absolute logical necessity; but
logic has, and logic emphatically asserts the existence
of it. Truth is possible, and therefore there is an
absolute and essential difference between truth and
falsehood. Therefore, there is an absolute and essential
rule and standard of truth. Therefore, there is, be it
abstract or be it concrete, an absolute and essential
logical necessity. Again, there is an essential distinction
between good and evil. There must, then, be an absolute and essential standard of right. Here some Atheists
get very restive. They are in a dilemma. If they deny
the existence of any absolute standard of right, they at
once and completely break with the most solemn and
sacred verdict of mankind on moral matters. They
deny the very first principle of morality. If they admit
the existence of an absolute standard of right, they cannot
deny the existence of Necessary Being. But a Necessary
Being is God. The more clever amongst them try to
escape by a compromise. They deny the principles of
Theism, and they deny the conclusions of Atheism.
They deny any real standard of right; yet, they deny

that they make no distinction between right and wrong. They call themselves Utilitarians, because they admit no good in anything except in so far as it is useful for something else. Consequently, they deny any real good or worth whatsoever in any thought or word or work of man. This is the plain truth. Some of them try to quibble out of it, but they cannot. They say that their rule of conduct runs practically over the same lines as ours, because what men admit to be morally good is most useful in the end. That is a dishonest shirking of the question. Is murder itself wrong? Is stealing in itself wrong? Is gratitude of itself good? Is filial affection good, independently of any utility? Yes or No. If there is any intrinsic difference between moral good and moral evil, there is some absolute standard of right. If there is no such intrinsic difference, then every sane man and woman is a lunatic, for, mark well, this is no mere abstract theory or scientific subtlety. Ordinary folk may easily get muddled over the Principle of Contradiction, but it is only fun or frenzy that ever makes them doubt it. Common-sense is infallible in its judgments of first principles. Those who rebel against its jurisdiction are logical outlaws. Now, the Principle of Contradiction in morality is the affirmation of the intrinsic reality of good, and the denial of its possible identification with evil. If there is no intrinsic difference between good and evil, it is vain to attempt to bolster up this sweeping condemnation of reason, with outside relations of usefulness. Usefulness in moral matters is impossible, if there be no intrinsic good or evil, because there is nothing for which it can be useful. Is there any standard of usefulness or not? If there is not, usefulness is impossible. If there is, it cannot be merely useful;

because usefulness cannot be merely of use to itself. If it is not merely useful, but worthy of pursuit for its own sake; then, the whole pack of Utilitarian cards tumbles down; for, we have got to something intrinsically good in itself and of itself. If this standard is variable, it is no standard. If it is invariable, it is absolute. If it is absolute, we have got what we want, an absolute standard of moral worth.

That there should be some absolute moral necessity, some rule superior to the whim or choice of human will, some standard to which men's minds should reasonably bow with reverence and which men's lives should realise by their own willing action, is, evidently and absolutely, needed to distinguish authority from tyranny, obedience from servility, and thus render social and civic life befitting the dignity of man, and thus put nations in their proper place above the herds of cattle, above the hordes of swine. Now, authority has no fit basis unless in the duty essentially owed to a supreme Power, and in the attraction exercised by an absolutely ultimate End.

Thus, the fact of order in the world of force, of truth, of worth, of inner and of outer human life, affirms the actual existence of a Necessary Principle without which it can be no fact at all.

Take away a self-sufficing principle of reality, a primal source of power, an inflexible rule of truth, an inviolable standard of good, a supreme law of right, an absolute aim and final crowning of will, what have you left? Not the world of fact; but the chaos of an Atheist. Given these, or any of these, what have we? The actual Existence of Necessary Being. Now, Necessary Being is God. Therefore, God exists.

Q.E.D.

Third Book

THE NATURE OF NECESSARY BEING

Third Book

CHAPTER I

THE ESSENCE OF NECESSARY BEING

We wish to come to a clear understanding as to the meaning of these two words, Nature and Essence. Essence we take to mean that which intrinsically constitutes a thing. We are not speaking of that which makes or fashions, or causes a thing; nor are we speaking of what is accidental; but we are speaking of what is innermost and most thoroughly identical with the thing itself. Essence is therefore called by the old philosophers "That by which a thing is what it is." Essence may be considered as it is in itself the internal constituent of Being, or it may be considered as it is a principle of activity, that is to say, in relation to its power of work. In the first case, Essence is simply called Essence. In the second case, Essence is called Nature. We will first speak about the Essence of Necessary Being. Then we shall have something to say about the attributes which follow from that Essence, and the powers logically deduced from it. We will group all these considerations under the name of the Nature of Necessary Being.

We must begin by drawing attention to the relations which exist between Essence and Existence. Existence is described as the act of Essence. In simpler English, Essence is the kind, Existence is the reality, of a thing.

Now the kind and the reality of a thing are not distinct in fact. They are logically distinct, because when a thing is merely possible, it has no reality in fact, and therefore no Existence, but, it is its own kind, and therefore is an Essence. A possible horse is not the same kind of thing as a possible cow. A possible horse is said to be made actual by reason of its Existence. Essence is therefore potential in relation to Existence. Existence is actual in relation to Essence. All this refers to Essence and Existence as considered in themselves. If they be considered with reference to our knowledge, some notion of the kind of a thing must be involved in any notion of its Existence. But the knowledge of its existence does not at all suppose anything like a thorough knowledge of its kind.

Up to the present we have been speaking about the Existence of God. We have supposed some sort of idea as to the Nature or Essence of God. But these ideas and notions were very vague. We have not attempted to prove the Existence of God, such as Christians believe Him to be, nor even such as most men know Him to be. We have been quite content to find out that there exists a Being with some such characteristic or other as shows Him to be quite above all other things. In fact we are most thoroughly satisfied if we have proved the Existence of a Necessary Being.

We will now examine the subordinate notions involved in the notion of Necessary Being. Necessary Being is a Being that must essentially exist. It is a Being the non-existence of which is impossible in physical fact, and an absurdity in logical thought. It would be as absolutely impossible that Necessary Being should not be, as that two and two should not make four. Now a Being that is necessary, must be necessary of and by and from itself. It cannot have got its Being from a cause, for then it would not itself be necessary. It must be necessary because it is Itself. Its Essence must include its necessity. As Necessary Being is of itself, its Existence must be identical with its Essence. Not only must its actual reality be thoroughly the same thing as its Essential kind, but even in logical thought, its essence must be thoroughly and completely identified with its Existence, to such a degree, that the mere consideration of its Essence, as distinct in thought from its Existence, would render that essence completely distinct from itself. Hence, in Necessary Being everything is Existence. Mark, we do not say that everything must be existent, because that might imply that its actuality could either come from some outside cause, or be a sort of attribute flowing outward from within; but we say that everything is Existence, because the inmost Essence which makes Necessary Being what it really is, is this, that it of its own self simply and essentially *Is*.

This definition exactly coincides with the definition given in Scripture of the nature of God: "I am Who am." The force of the Hebrew words cannot be given in English. The Hebrew "Am" is not in the present tense as we would say, for the Hebrews do not distinguish their tenses, with reference to time. Their tenses refer to the finishing of an act or to its continuance. The Hebrew "Am" means the continuance of the Existence of a Being Who is the continuance of the act of Existence. Hence the first essential notion of Necessary Being is that it is of itself. The notion immediately following on this is that Necessary Being is Existence.

CHAPTER II

THE INFINITY OF NECESSARY BEING

NECESSARY Being must be perfect. It must have everything that it is possible for it to have, and whatever it has not must be impossible to it. Hence, if anything could possibly be added to it, this addition need not of necessity exist, and consequently could not possibly belong to Necessary Being. In other words, in Necessary Being, Necessity and Being are logically co-extensive, so that, in affirmation and in negation they are thoroughly interchangeable. Therefore Necessary Being must have of itself, most perfectly realised within itself, all perfection that is possible to it; therefore Necessary Being is perfect.

Now this perfection of Necessary Being has no limit. Were any limit possible in its perfection, this limit must either be set by some outside cause, or it must be the result of the very Essence of Necessary Being itself. Now Necessary Being cannot have any limit set to it from outside. For, being perfectly independent, and wholly and entirely from and of itself, it is superior to all exterior action, and quite beyond the control of any agent other than itself. Neither can any limit be set to Necessary Being by the kind of its own nature. In all creatures nature has its own limit. The very nature of matter excludes intellectual power. The very nature of intellect excludes material substance. Even the highest perfections in creatures, by the very fact of their own being, stop short somewhere in the ascent towards supreme good. But in Necessary Being this is not so. Its perfection is its very own, and essentially requires for its very own every perfection possible to it. Now all perfection is possible to it. The only limit set to itself by Necessary Being is the limit set by its own necessity of self-existence. Now this excludes nothing that is perfectly compatible with Being. It excludes everything incompatible with Being. It excludes whatever is bound up with contingency, or imperfection, or failure, or defect. It excludes whatever is opposed to perfection, and whatever falls short of perfection. Hence, in its own order of being, a Necessary Being is an existence so boundless, as to own with thorough identity, whatever can of necessity exist. But perfect perfection, while it is impossible to contingent Being, is quite possible to Necessary Being; for, in Necessary Being there is no limit to perfection except the limit of self-existence. This limit is in reality no limit in positive affirmation of Being. It is only a limit in as far as it is a positive denial of Non-Being.

Briefly, Necessary Being is infinite, because it can neither have any limit set to its perfection by another, nor is there any limit set to its perfection by its own nature. Its nature is necessary and therefore independent. Its nature is existence and therefore boundless.

There is scarcely any need to add that this Infinity of which we speak, is not an infinity of multitude, but an Infinity, the intensity of which does not take from its simplicity, and the extent of which in no wise lessens its unity.

CHAPTER III

UNITY OF NECESSARY BEING

THERE are two ways in which we may prove the Unity of Necessary Being. We may prove it directly from its necessity, or by its infinity.

In the last Chapter we have proved that Necessary Being is infinite. Now this cannot mean that Necessary Being is identical with all sorts of Being; for we have also proved that Necessary Being excludes all that is contingent and imperfect. Therefore the infinity of Necessary Being essentially excludes the possibility of its being identical with creatures. But, in its own order, Necessary Being is simply everything. Whatever perfection is possible in an absolute and unlimited degree, belongs to the order of Necessary Being, and whatever belongs to the order of Necessary Being, comes within reach of the possibility of one Necessary Being. Therefore, one Necessary Being, as it is infinite, is all Necessary Being and therefore only one.

The second proof of the Unity of Necessary Being is drawn directly from the necessity of its existence. Its existence is its very essence, and therefore essentially includes whatever is necessary for actual existence. Now, individuality is necessary for existence, because a thing cannot exist, unless it is some particular individual thing. Therefore, Necessary Being essentially owns individuality. Therefore Necessary Being is essentially an individual.   Therefore Necessary Being is essentially only one.   Mark well that this individuality cannot be an abstract individuality; for we are not speaking of a Being that may be merely possible, we are speaking of a Being that cannot but be a fact.   Hence, this individuality of Necessary Being is as particular and definite as the individuality of any fact.   Hence, Necessary Being can no more be anything but one particular individual, than any existing fact can be a different thing from itself. Mark also, that when we say that individuality is essential to Necessary Being, we must mean that this individuality is as identical, not only really, but also logically, with the inmost essence of Necessary Being, as with its own existence or its own Essence.

Briefly, Unity, in the sense of actual downright individuality, is identical with the very inmost essence of Necessary Being.   Wherefore, were we to suppose any number of Necessary Beings possible, as their abstract essence would be the same, so their actual physical identity in fact would be the same, and so they would be all identically the one sole, Necessary Being; therefore, Necessary Being must essentially be one and only one.

CHAPTER IV

ETERNITY OF NECESSARY BEING

WE all have an idea of what Time is, but very few
have correct notions on the matter. It is not that
people are mistaken, rather they do not think deeply
enough about it to come to any thought-out conclusion.
Hence, although what we are about to say will seem in
one way very new, in another way it will sound like the
voice of an old friend. Time is defined by Aristotle to
be "The measure of Movement." Of course all young
people will at once quarrel with this definition. Let
them reflect first a little more. Aristotle gives a very
subtle definition of Movement. He calls it "The act of
potential Being in so much as it is potential." Movement, according to our ordinary way of speaking and
thinking, is taken to express the passing from one place
to another. There is something analogous to this in all
activity, in all evolution, in all that, in whatsoever way,
begins or ends. We want some one word to express one
idea that is common to all change. Movement is a good
word for this, because in its deep and wide meaning it
conveys the idea of a passing from one point to another,
and so is verified also in the passing from one degree to
another, in the passing from one state to another, in the
passing from anything to anything. Movement is not
the arriving at the term or goal whither the moving
object tends. Neither is Movement a starting or be-

ginning. Movement is the transit. Yet Movement is not the transit in so far as there is some space already got over, for that would be considering Movement as ended, and hence as no Movement. But, Movement means the transit in so far as the body is actually going further, and, by reason of this actual tending, onwards. When this is put in an universal manner, it is best expressed by taking two words which divide all Being, Being as complete, and Being as incomplete. These words are, *actual* and *potential*. Thus in as far as a Being is actual it is in the term or goal of Movement. In as far as a Being is potential it is in the starting-point of Movement. In so far as it is actually going from the starting-point to its term, and as it is actually going onward, it is said to be that kind of actuality which there is in potential Being, in so far as this potentiality is becoming actualized. This is Aristotle's definition of Movement.

The measure of Movement is not taken to be a measure in intensity, as though we were measuring the perfection or actuality which exists in the body that starts to move. Rather it is the movement in extent, or the measure in so far as it relates to the relation of passing from start to term.

Wherefore the measure of Movement taken in this way is a thorough definition of Time.

Perhaps it would seem strange, but it is very true, to say that Time in its usual acceptation is only an external or exterior relation. There are two kinds of Time, the one extrinsic, the other intrinsic. Extrinsic Time is the measure of movement decided according to an exterior rule or standard. Thus, when you look at your watch after a long walk, you may say that you have made a good record, having got over twenty miles in four hours. What is the real meaning of this? It means that you have moved a distance of twenty miles while the hands of your watch were moving round a certain space. This means further that you have done your twenty miles during one-sixth of the measure of the daily movement of the earth around the sun. In reality different things change and move with different rapidities. For this reason, in human life we take some one particular movement which is obvious to all, and uniform, as a standard whereby to gauge the movements of other things. Wherefore the time of day means the comparison between any other particular movement, and the movement, as in our ordinary way we say, of the daily course of the sun.

Intrinsic Movement is the Movement which is actually taking place in anything. Thus the change which is ceaselessly going on in the life of a man, in the growing of a tree, in the springing of the corn, in the floating of the clouds, in the running of the stream, in the crumbling of the rock, in the formation of coal, or in the deepening of a desire: this is intrinsic Time. If its changes are abrupt it is a Time made up of instants, unlike the time we usually speak of. If it flows continuously, taking in duration the same place which is taken in space by quantity, this is, strictly speaking, Time. Just as in a certain length there are, or may be, parts and points without number, not actualized, but potential, so that they all coalesce into one measurement in space; so in duration, the parts and points of Time are spread out so as like one moving point to make one spread-out duration.

Duration may be defined to be Continuance in Exist-

ence. The nature of duration in so far as it is intrinsic,
depends on the Being that exists.   In material Being as
the nature is made up of matter, and so exists under the
form of continuous quantity, so its duration flows in a
continuous manner, and is therefore, strictly speaking, a
duration of time. This is not the case in all things.
Thus, if we take a thought as it is in itself, there is nothing
to prevent its remaining in fixed and motionless gaze on
its object, during durations that would correspond to
very widely different external measurements of material
movement. A thought may come and go like a flash.
But while an intellectual thought dwells in the mind, it
does not change in itself. It is an indivisible instant.
We may call it a mathematical instant of duration.
Yet, again, a thought may abide in one steady, yet
identical, permanence of existence. This also is an
instant, a mathematical instant of intellect. If we
compare these two instants according to our external
standard of Time, they will differ much.   If we compare
them, in themselves, we can find no intrinsic ground of
proportion; for each such instant is perfectly present to
itself, perfectly identical throughout itself, wholly and
thoroughly spiritual. However, the succession of spiritual, or, as we may call them, angelic instants, makes up
a kind of Time.   But it is a Time, the units of which are
actually distinct and quite unequal and uneven.   It is a
succession which may in some way be compared to a
collection of figures of different value.   In the existence
of Necessary Being there is duration, but there is no
succession, there is no change. All that can be in
Necessary Being is simultaneous, and all-complete.
Therefore in Necessary Being there is no such thing as
Time, nor can there be.

The existence of Necessary Being is its very essence. Its essence is that by which it is what it is. It cannot cease to be what it is, nor can it cease to own that by which it essentially is its own essential self. Therefore all its existence is intensified into one simple yet infinite, single yet boundless, one yet never-failing instant. Its duration is Eternity. Eternity has been described by Boetius as "The whole simultaneous and perfect owning of life that has no term." Necessary Being owns its own existence, for it is its very essence. It owns this existence perfectly, because it is of and from and by itself alone. It owns this existence all at once, because the necessity of its Being excludes the possibility of gain or loss. It owns this existence, all of it, because it is all identical with itself. This existence is without term, because it is infinite. Wherefore, the existence of Necessary Being is one utter and infinite instant that unites the Always of the past, and the Always of the future in the same indivisible, identical, and living Now. Wherefore, Necessary Being is Eternal.

CHAPTER V

PERSONALITY OF NECESSARY BEING

FROM the knowledge of finite facts, we can get to the knowledge of a First Principle that is infinite. This First Principle is the source of all reality, the standard of all truth, and the bourne of all tendency. We have got so far in our knowledge of what Necessary Being is, as to understand that we must deny of it all imperfection, because imperfection is bound up with limitation, and consequently with finite nature. We also understand that we must affirm of Necessary Being all pure perfection; because firstly, no cause can give what it has not got itself; because secondly, Necessary Being is the Principle of Possibility; because thirdly, the nature of Necessary Being requires that it should be only Being, that is, only Reality and all Reality which is simply and absolutely such, and so, not bounded by anything within the widest expanse of such Reality as is unmixed with unreality. Although we have got to such a high idea of God, we have got to it by the way of denial, rather than by the way of positive affirmation. As Denis the Areopagite says: "We rather know what God is not, than what He is." This brings us in front of the primal notion by which we separate God from Creatures. When speaking of those things which we meet with in our own universe, we measure their perfection by the grades of Being which they include. Thus we speak of the nature of lifeless things. When we would reach to a higher region we add to this notion, the notion of life, and we have the added perfection of vegetation. To this we may again add the notion of sensible knowledge and feeling. This brings us up to animal life. If we add further to this the notion of intellectual ideas, we have got to the grade of rational existence. It seems plain that starting from the first notion of Being, the more grades we gather of perfection, the higher will be the nature we realise. But, all this rests upon the supposition that Being is the same in all things. This supposition is true, when we speak of Being that is finite, Contingent, and therefore dependent. If we begin by completely altering our very notion of Being, we find ourselves in another sphere. If we take, not finite, Contingent, dependent Being, but Being, that is its own Being, that is utterly and in every way independent Being that is Necessary, then we have a full and final means of separating such Being from all other things that may or may not be. This notion of Necessary is one that cannot be added to by an accumulation of prerogatives. It is one that requires only to have its inherent infinity explained. Hence it is that while we explain the nature of finite things by giving the different degrees by which they are separated from nothingness; when speaking of God we give all that can be given of His nature and Essence, by giving the true notion of what His mere existence means. Thus as we have explained, the Essence of Necessary Being is in its own complete and utter owning of itself; in the fact of its being of itself, by itself, self-sufficing. From this it follows the notion of Being is not applied in the same way to God as to Creatures. It is said of them analogically, that is to say, the very idea of Being is realised in each in a different way. It is not merely that their Being is different. It is not merely that a difference is added on to their Being. But the very idea of Being itself, is intrinsically differentiated as it is applied to one, or to the other. Being, primarily and of itself, belongs to Necessary Being. It is only dependently and in a secondary way that Being can be applied to things which owe both their possibility and their actuality to the fact of their dependence on Being that is of itself.

These thoughts will have already answered in the most full and complete manner questions which might be asked as to the nature of God. It is the fashion amongst poor scribblers who love to write about deep questions because they are quite familiar with surface subjects, to speak of the Great Being as though He were nothing more than *It*. They write wildly about Nature of Necessity, but they fail to understand the A. B. C. of a nature that is Necessary. In the fact of Necessary Being there is incomparably more given than any Atheist would think a Theist should be called upon to prove. It is simple and absolute infinitude. It is first and final power. It is utter and measureless perfection. This more than proves that Necessary Being is intellectual. It is intellectual because it is all-perfect. It is intellectual because it is the source, the exemplar, and the type of all intellectual as well as material possibility. It is intellectual because its essence is its own most thorough actuality.

The intellectuality of Necessary Being is, in the first place, evident from this: that it is possible for Necessary Being to be intellectual, therefore it is intellectual. We have seen above that Necessary Being essentially owns all perfection that is possible to it, and that whatever is excluded from it, is excluded by reason of its very Essence. Now, that a Necessary Being should be intellectual, is not absurd. A Being that is eternally and infinitely self-owned and self-existent is very much more susceptible of intelligence than you are yourself; yet you would scarcely deny that you might possibly be intellectual.

Again, Necessary Being is the first type and first cause of all things that are. It is then the type and cause of all thought that is true, and of all knowledge that is thorough. This shows plainly that it is itself capable of knowledge, and therefore intellectual.

Lastly, Necessary Being is utterly actual. It is then in no way potential. Therefore it is not material, for material Being is essentially potential. Is it then spiritual? It is only spiritual in such a sense as to be at the same time most substantial in its essence and most actual in its existence. This renders it most perfectly present to itself, in a much more perfect sense than thought could be to mind. As its faculties cannot be distinct from its very essence, so neither can its act or its action be distinct from itself. Therefore its own very essence being thoroughly actual, and being thoroughly identical with its faculty, it must be conscious; for consciousness is the thorough self-presence of an actualized spiritual Being with itself. Consciousness is the inherent self-knowledge bound up with the reflection of a being that can think. Consciousness requires not merely presence in space, but presence in identity of Being. It also requires that the spiritual power of thought should be actual. Now Necessary Being as it is perfectly identical through and through with all that is in itself, and as it is the most actual determination that all self-existence can have, is, up to the very highest limits of possible perfection, actual Being.

Intellectual Beings are persons. This we need not prove. The most elementary notion of what a person is, is bound up with the ideas of thought and will. Therefore in Necessary Being the perfection of its thought and will is as absolute in intensity and extent, as the perfectness of its Nature.

Therefore Necessary Being is a Person. Therefore Necessary Being must be recognised as the Personality of God.

CHAPTER VI

KNOWLEDGE OF GOD

THE fact of Knowledge is easily admitted; the nature of Knowledge is not easily understood. When you say that you know something, what do you really mean? You must mean this: that the object known, exists in an intellectual manner within your thought. Let us try to analyse this. Thought is a likeness. This likeness cannot be merely the likeness of a photograph. The paper on which the sun determines an image, cannot be said to know the object which it represents. There must be some peculiar way in which what is known is lifted up to be born to intellectual existence within the mind that knows it. First, let us take the object which is to be known. If we were merely to speak of that kind of knowledge which is possessed by sense-faculties, we should circumscribe the kind of objects which are suitable to be known by each. The eye cannot see sound, nor can the ear listen to colour. But when there is question of intellect, whatever is true is, in so far, of itself knowable. We have got all we require on the part of the object. Now let us analyse the conditions requisite on the side of mind. Mind is its own self, and therefore, of course, an identical image of itself. Being spiritual, it is most thoroughly present in identity of substance with itself. It is not merely in the same place; it is thoroughly and truly, through and through the self-same

indivisible substance. If its nature is sufficiently actualized as to be able to act, it is self-conscious; for its
own image is intellectually present within itself. Furthermore, spiritual Being, while remaining its own true
self, can receive within itself secondary and accidental
images of other things. It does not require for this to
cease to be in any way its own self. It merely requires
to be able in an intellectual manner to reproduce an
intellectual representation of an intellectual or intellectualized object. In order that any outward object should
be known, the power which intellect has of knowing
anything, must be practically and immediately determined to know, that is, intellectually to represent, some
definite and particular thing. Now, if we suppose that
an intellectual object acts upon an intellectual subject,
we may also naturally suppose that such determination
being of a kind kindred to the source from which it
comes, will produce a determination kindred to its kind,
when it reaches the knowing subject. On receiving this
determination, the knowing subject reacts, giving mental
birth to the mental likeness which is conceived. If the
mind which knows, is sufficiently and of itself, determined
to know certain objects, it will not require any actual
action on the part of the objects in order that it should be
determined to know them. If it be supposed that an
intellect is of its own nature actually and ultimately
determined to actual knowledge of all truth, there will
be no need, nor indeed any possibility of its receiving any
impression from without. Now this is the case with
Necessary Being. Having all perfection that is possible
for it to have, it is of itself actually determined to know
all that is knowable. Being infinite in its own actual
perfection, its power of knowing extends as widely in

extent, and reaches as high in intensity, as stretches or reaches the knowableness of truth. That anything should be knowable and therefore known to Necessary Being, it is sufficient that it should be true. Thus truth is the only condition, as it is the only limit of the Knowledge possessed by Necessary Being.

CHAPTER VII

WILL OF NECESSARY BEING

It appears evident that Will follows on Intellect. We
cannot wish for what we do not know. But can our Will
be exercised with regard to any object that is known?
This too seems plain; but we have to get to the reason
for it. The first reason which meets us on the threshold,
is that as thought sets an object before us showing moreover what is good or evil, desirable or odious, in it, the
Will, which is the faculty by which we determine ourselves to action, may or must as the case may be, choose
or leave that object. This reason is not final. How is it
that Will can like or dislike what is known? There is a
deeper reason to be given. Everything that is, acts
according to its kind. When, then, an object comes by
thought into intellectual existence within our mind, it
has there a definite action, not only on our faculty of
comprehension, but also on the faculty which moves us
to seek for what is good to us and to avoid what is evil.
Wherefore, the image of the object within our soul is the
means by which that object draws or repels us. According to the nature of the object this attraction or repulsion
may be greater or less. In some cases it may be inevitable. Why it is that the Will can seek or shun what
the intellect knows, is explained by the nature of the
faculty. The intellect is the comprehensive faculty of
the soul, the Will is the expansive faculty. Each cor-

responds with the other as a twin form of spiritual action. The measure of comprehension is the measure of expansion both in kind and in degree. The comprehension is necessary, because truth is absolute. The expansion is also necessary towards an adequate object, because such object is its absolute good. The expansion is not necessary although it is possible towards any object that is not its adequate object, because such object is relative good. The expansion of Necessary Being is, in the first place, and of necessity, towards itself, for, It is Itself the only object thoroughly worthy of Its own love. Yet as It infinitely comprehends all things that are, or may be, so Its Will may freely stoop from its infinite dignity to lift them up by loving them. God's Will is free, for no creature is necessary to Him, nor can any creature add to His perfection or His pleasure. These latter must be exclusively complete within the Creator's own order of Existence. This freedom is not the untroubled quiet of selfishness. It is rather the essential condition for that overflowing and unrequited benevolence by which God, Who cannot gain anything for Himself, gives His love, and by His love makes all things that are true and good, lovable.

CHAPTER VIII

POWER OF GOD

In all things which we know, power of acting follows on the kind of the Being that acts, not only as to the sort of work that may be done, but also as to its possible intensity or degree. Indeed, it would appear almost useless to say that Power is proportioned to Nature. All physical sciences rely on this fact, that we may judge of what kind things are, from the way in which they act. The nature of God being infinite, there can be no limit to His Power. He cannot do what is impossible, because what is impossible is simply and absolutely nothing, and it would be absurd to suppose that any Power could act and yet do nothing. Again, the range of possibility is defined by the measure in which the essence of God can be represented or imitated by things outside Himself. Thus, God is the first Principle of Possibility, and His power is co-equal with this primal foundation of Possibility, and therefore His power can do, whatever is in any way or in any sense possible to be done.

We, who are finite creatures, stopping far short of perfection, need, in order to carry out our wish, to set in motion subordinate powers that are destined for immediate physical use. Thus even when I form the wish and resolve to twirl my moustache, I am obliged, in order to effect this, to set my fingers to it. If my will were still more actual, and if whatever in any way belonged to me depended immediately and solely on my wish, my very wish would be sufficient of itself to produce any result which now I can produce only by other means. In Necessary Being Will is omnipotent, Will is absolute, Will is physical cause; and therefore Will alone and of itself, by its supreme *fiat* and by its resistless decree, makes or unmakes, as it lists.

Fourth Book
A TRIPLE TOUCHSTONE

Fourth Book

CHAPTER I

FREE-WILL

THE manner in which a man treats the questions of Free-Will, the Origin of Evil, and Hell, is an accurate test of the temper in which he will approach the question of the Existence of God. If he admits Free-Will, or if he explains the Origin of Evil without any unpleasant "isms," or if he does not get angry at the mention of Hell, he may be counted on to admit the Existence of God when this is put fairly before him. If he denies the fact of Free-Will, the possibility of Hell, and any Origin of Evil that is not fatalist or fiendish, you must not expect him to retain arguments contrary to his craze until he is restored to a healthy tone of mind. He must be treated, logically, as a sick mind. If a man settles down into doubt on these points, it will be found that he is given to refusing any recognition to facts or principles when he gets puzzled over their explanation or consequences. He will get safely to the truth, if he keep rigorously to strict logical sequence in reasoning, and never take a further step until he is secure on the spot where he stands.

We begin with Free-Will. What kind of people deny Free-Will? They are not all of the same sort. There is a very potent motive underneath the outside principles

which decorate some human lives. It is not quite unknown in the world that a man should follow a certain
course of conduct, and yet try to shirk the responsibility
of it by sailing under false colours. Adam threw the
blame on Eve. Eve threw the blame on the Serpent.
Some bad boys throw the blame on the absence of Free-
Will. It is very convenient; but it is very mean.

Again, there are intellectual cranks. A man who
denies Free-Will is unable to look at life like anybody
else. He must sweep aside with one prodigious denial
the universal principles and the universal practice of
common-sense. He must set down the universal moral
sense of mankind as utter foolery or arrant superstition.
Worst of all, in his own conduct, if it is to be honourable,
he must contradict his own principles.

We lock up lunatics, even though they consider that
we ought to change places with them. A few men say
to the entire human race: "From our heart, we pity
you. You not only do not know what you are saying;
you do not know what you are thinking. It is very sad,
but you are a pack of fools. You are all mad on the
simplest fact in the world. You think that you are free.
Of course we act as if we thought so too, but we don't,
and you mustn't. You are lunatics and we are sane."

Is mankind mad, or are some of our self-sent Prophets
only monomaniacs? Reflect that if you deny Free-Will,
you must admit a great deal of nonsense, and tolerate a
vast amount of bad conduct.

Who admit Free-Will? Every man with a good
heart, two straight eyes, and a hard fist, knows right
well that he has a will of his own. Every woman, who
has the heart of a woman, knows that she has the power
of a woman to be a redeemer of men. She knows that

she has the will, the wayward will it may be, but the blessed will of a woman, that can lift up those she loves. Men and women know when sober, and will tell you when they are sincere, that if they choose they can say either yes or no. Speaking roundly, men and women who believe in God, admit Free-Will; and men and women who admit Free-Will, when they are willing to let conclusions force themselves upon them, admit God.

It is not right to say that because a truth is convenient or pleasant, therefore we must hold it to be true. But on the other hand, when we recognise a truth to be true, when we have examined and understood the proofs of it, then, a new and exquisite light may dawn upon the old truths, which to us were household truths before. Thus the truth of the existence of God comes with an admirable and vivid splendour, to consecrate every high principle, every noble aspiration, every great aim, every glorious undertaking of man's life. It is like the sunshine that is reflected back again from things, of their own nature fitted to receive the light.

Come to the point. Let us talk about Free-Will. What is Free-Will? or what do these words mean? We hold that there is a faculty in our being which can seek for good. We hold that we can wish for something, that we can desire something, that we can love something. This outward tendency of our being, this leaning forward, this need of something more, this craving, this thirst, this wishing, we call the faculty of Will. We call the act by which it actually wills to have something, a wish. Is Will free? Will is not free in its final impulse. It is the outward tendency of the whole being, it is the want within a nature of what shall make this nature in itself complete, and by the possession of its object, happy.

There is no question of the primal impulse, the fundamental desire of Will. We do not say that any man can
wish to be miserable; we do not say that any man can
give up the hope of happiness. Some atheistic philosophers apparently think that the advocates of Free-Will
leave everything free. What we do mean is this, that in
ordinary life, with regard to the ordinary actions and
usual determinations which occur in human life, men have
the power of choosing for themselves, of themselves,
and by themselves, whether they will do so or no. I say,
and every Cockney says, that if he likes to spend his
penny, he may go by the 'bus, and, if he chooses, he may
walk. Every Cockney knows and I know too, and you
know too, that you can walk, or if you have got the
penny, travel by the 'bus. Is it a fact or not? Does
everybody know that it is a fact? Does anybody doubt
of its being a fact? Certainly not! Nobody doubts it.
Did you ever hear the story of the old philosopher who
proved to a man that he could not walk? The man was
unable to answer the objection. He was completely
overwhelmed by the logic. It was made quite evident
to him that it was utterly and absolutely impossible
for him to walk, because walking is movement, and
movement is impossible. Was our friend convinced?
He was as most readers of modern reviews may be.
What did he do? He simply got up and walked. Is
Free-Will a fact? Don't you know it is? There is no
use in trying to quibble about the explanation of the
fact. We do not now want any explanation. A fact
does not need further explanation in order to be admitted
as a fact. A fact is a fact. Free-Will is a fact. Every-
one knows it is a fact. Will you hold to common-sense
or not?

We must expose a trick which wits, consciously or unconsciously sportive, sometimes turn against Free-Will. "You cannot but do as you like best to do. Therefore, what pleases you most, is inevitable. Therefore you can't help doing it. Therefore you have no choice." What do you mean by "Like best?" Do you mean, "You cannot but elect to do what is most pleasing to you before you make your choice?" If so, the statement is quite false. Do you mean, "You cannot but do what you actually choose to do?" If so, the statement is quite true; but the determination towards one side or the other is consequent on the choice of Free-Will, not antecedent to it. In the difficulty, the second meaning is hung out, and then the first meaning is substituted for it.

There is a clear and strong proof of Free-Will to be drawn from the nature of its dependence upon intellect. We cannot wish for what we do not know. Thought is the measure of wish, in so far, at least, as to be a necessary condition for the action of Will. We need not suppose that intellect and will are distinct faculties in the way in which the sense of sight and the sense of hearing are distinct. Yet we must at least speak of them as having different characteristic features. The intellect is that power of the soul by which it can know things. Will is a power following upon the first, by which the soul is enabled to wish for what it knows. Thought puts before Will the object of this latter. Now the action which an object shall have upon Will, must depend on the way in which it is represented in thought. If before the soul there should be evidently set an object so great and good, as to have in it no possible flaw, no failing in perfection, then the Will would be unable to refuse to love that object. The Will is made to seek for what is shown to be good to it, and to shun what is seen to be evil. The Will cannot but love good, nor can it but hate evil, as such. If the object be all good, and only good, there is no motive for repulsion; if the object be only evil, or only seen under the aspect of evil, there is no motive in it for attraction. If an object is by intellect so set before the will, as to be distinctly visible both as good in one respect, and as evil in some other way, then there is sufficient motive power for the will either to seek or to avoid it. Looking at things from the side of the object, we have here an actual indifference in the judgment passed by intellect upon the object's worth. It is decreed that the object is not of necessity to be loved nor of necessity to be hated. It is made evident that the object may be loved or may be hated. We have here a reasonable ground for Free-Will to act on. We have the objective indifference in the manner in which the object is by thought set before the Will. If you say that the Will must yield to whichever motive is the stronger, you say much more than reason says. Reason does not present the object in any such guise. Reason presents the object as susceptible both of love and of hate. On the side of the faculty of Will we must have an energy that is, of itself, and by its own inherent nature, ready to act. The will does not require to be made complete before it acts. Mind, indeed, in order to give birth to knowledge, must be determined by the seed of truth, which is the likeness of the object. But will needs no such determination. Will is of itself thoroughly prepared. It is the actual energy of the soul directed towards good. It only needs that the object be by knowledge set before it, in order that it may seek the good, and shun the evil, according to the way in which these are made evident. That a faculty should be able to determine its own self in one way or in another, is not hard to understand. We must admit that in this case the will actually has, at the same time, both the power of willing and the power of not willing to seek the object. We say that the two powers must co-exist in the will. We do not say that the two actions can be exerted at the same time. Now when will has at the same time the power of choosing and the power of leaving what is offered to it, its use of liberty consists in the fact of the will doing one thing which it certainly can do, and yet not doing another thing which although it could have done, there was no necessity that it should do. Briefly, from the way in which any finite object is set before the will, this latter faculty has a reasonable objective motive, on both sides of the question, each one of which motives is quite enough to enable it to act, yet not enough to force it. Thus the faculty of will can use its own energy, under the guidance of thought, to turn one way rather than another. This is Free-Will.

Those who deny Free-Will have a very big difficulty to face. Do they deny its possibility, or do they not? If they do not deny the possibility of it, all their rational arguments against Free-Will fall to the ground, and they have no arguments drawn from experience, for all men say that experience plainly proves the contrary. It is all very well for them to say that other people are mistaken, and are incapable of judging of what passes within themselves. This is too much of a good thing. Very few people are capable of explaining, much less of proving, the nature of their own mental acts, but all men are quite capable, if they are sane and sober, of getting just far enough to simply state some obvious and frequent facts that happen within their own consciousness. The human race has unanimously declared that Free-Will is a downright fact. This is very strong evidence from personal experience. If there is no metaphysical argument to break it down, it looks a sufficiently solid barrier to set against Determinatists. Do they then deny the possibility of Free-Will? They have not yet attempted to give any proof worth quoting of such a doctrine. In order to succeed, they should prove that it is absurd to suppose a spiritual power active enough, when its object is set before it, to determine itself without being necessitated thereunto. That within the same faculty of the soul there should co-exist both the power of choosing one course and the power of choosing the opposite course, makes no additional difficulty; for these two powers, as such, are not at all opposed to one another. To attempt to prove that Free-Will is impossible, is making too large a demand on any one's credulity. If this be not evidently proved, the opponents of Free-Will have no real claim to be listened to.

CHAPTER II

THE ORIGIN OF EVIL

The good of material Creatures, and their harmonious co-existence in the universe, require that there should be change. Order amongst things whose nature is essentially passing, needs that there should be a constant action and reaction of one thing upon another. Now action and reaction that are real, and change that is not mere appearance, mean that what was, should cease to be, and that what now is not, should yet come to be. Hence the perfection of material things is bound up with their ceaseless building up of themselves. And yet their highest use depends upon the fact that they can be destroyed. The grass that is most fresh and tender is the best, not merely because of its brilliant green, but more so because by it, nobler beings than itself can live. If the grass were indestructible, it would be a very inconvenient investment for any unfortunate cow. But it is no good to the grass that it should be eaten. As far as good or evil can be applied to lifeless beings, the highest good of the grass is in the ultimate evil by which all its good ceases altogether to be. The highest good of the grass is in its usefulness, but its usefulness is in its death. Physical evil is therefore an essential part of the good of the material universe. The good of individuals is in their existence. Their evil is in their destruction. But their destruction is needed for the order of the universe, and thus becomes a higher good. This same law of the essential existence of evil obtains also amongst living things. According to the necessary rules of physical action, animals must grow from birth to maturity and then sink to decay. The fulness of their health and strength must bring them pleasure. The penalty of their weakness or inertness is pain. Their term of life may be long or short, but the good order of the world requires that the face of the earth should be renewed. The inexorable justice of physical force will not tolerate that useless, worked-out machines should encumber the globe. The winter that kills the flowers and leaves, is as good and useful as the Spring that brings new verdure to replace the old. So too in the animal world it cannot be that a field should be for ever sacrificed to the decrepid uselessness of an immortal ass. Good, beauty, strength, order, as they exist among Creatures made up of matter, essentially need the existence of evil. Wherefore not only is physical evil a necessary evil, but without it physical good would be impossible. What is evil? It is the absence of a good that is required. It is not the mere absence of good; for everything finite stops short in good, and is therefore without a higher good. But evil is the privation of good, that is to say, it is the absence of a good that is needed, of something that is really wanted, of something without which the thing in question positively falls short of the perfection due to its kind. Thus it is an evil for a cow to have only one horn, for every properly appointed cow should have two, much more is it an evil for a horse to be blind, or for a dog to have only three legs. It is an evil for a pig to be made bacon of, and it is an evil to wasps that they should be murdered when they only sting. It is evident that what in itself, within its own narrow sphere, is evil, may take its place in a higher scale of order as a real good. Hence physical evil in the case of individual units, may be a necessary part of physical good in the whole order of creation. Thus the order which exists amongst lifeless things, serves both by its good and evil to work out the order which exists amongst things that live. Much more does evil become in reality a good when the hurt or harm, or death, which happens in the physical order, works out the nobler good of order in the moral world. Pain is indeed an Evil, and poverty; yet many a time, in many a human heart, these sad seeds of bitterness brought forth rich and beautiful harvests of help that was devoted, and of love that was staunch. After all, those whose hair is white with age and grief, and whose brows with all their deep drawn furrows are yet crowned with patient calm, realise, when looking back over long dreary years, that it was not always the sunshine which brought them truest happiness, nor was it always the laugh or the joke that made the music which now finds the sweetest echo in their memory. Sorrow is often a blessing, and pain is very often the tender touch of the fatherly hand of God. Wretched mortals who are so shortsighted and so stupid, how can we understand all the magnificent interweaving of helping aid and chastening shock, all the infinite working out through infinite detail of the plan of the great Ruler of men!

What is sin? Sin is evil in the moral world. It means something done or undone which violates the supreme order of moral worth. Is sin possible? It is a fact. Is its possibility a necessity? Yes. The necessity for sin's possibility is identical with the necessity for the possibility of moral good. Moral good is impossible unless sin is possible. Why should this be so? Simply because moral good is impossible without free choice, and free choice is impossible without the possibility of sin. It is absurd to imagine that there can be any merit or worth in what is done under inevitable and absolute compulsion. If there is any ground for praise or honour, it must be only because the act which is praised or honoured is to be attributed to the person from whom it came. Now if that person had no more to do with the choice of that action, than a flower has to do with its colour or a metal with its weight, then that praise, that honour, is mockery. But if that person really did that deed, if it was his own doing, if it was his own choice, then he must have had the choice of doing it, he must have had the power of refusing it, he must have had the possibility of doing wrong.

The question as to the Origin of Evil has really nothing to do with the question of the existence of God. Whether sin be possible or not, whether God can or cannot allow sin, does not undermine or shake the fundamental and absolute necessity for the Existence of Necessary Being. Furthermore, the fact of Free-Will is also the fact of the possibility of moral Evil; just as the possibility of a material world involves the necessity of physical Evil. What really is attacked by those who busy themselves so very much about the Origin of Evil, is, not the Existence of God, but the nature; not the fact, but the attribute of God. Now we can meet all such arguments with one broad sweep of proof. If an intellectual Being is possible, Free-Will is possible. If Free-Will is possible, sin is possible. If sin is possible, the Origin of Evil is essentially to be explained by the essential nature of things. It cannot in any way be set down to the arbitrary will of God as to its sole cause. Hence that God should permit evil or allow sin is only one way of saying in detail what we say in a more general manner when we lay down as a most evident and admirable truth, that it is the wise and good decree of the All-Powerful not to mar but to make the world, not to destroy but to develop nature, not from without to work things against their own inmost needs, but through their own inborn and peculiar strivings, to work out a universal order.

As to why God should permit sin, we must first say this: God must, according to the Eternal laws of wisdom, permit His intellectual creatures to work out their own moral worth. But the working out of their own moral worth by themselves under God, is impossible, unless God also give them the power of committing sin. Yet, as far as is possible without crushing the liberty of doing good, God does prevent sin. All the power of His moral influence, His Commands, His law, His revelation, His threats, His entreaties, all these are set against sin. Moral force, such as is dazzling in its sublimity, and terrifying in its intensity, is set against sin. Still more, even the sanction of physical force follows on the footsteps of moral influence, so that the dread realities of a future physical doom cast their warning shadows into the present, to drive man back from sin. What more could God do to prevent sin? One thing more He could do, He could take away Free-Will. But that would destroy moral good, and the Existence of moral good is the only reason for the Existence of the world. Thus if God did not permit sin, He could not create the Universe. Such a permission cannot in any sense whatsoever be taken as an approval of sin.

CHAPTER III

HELL

WHEN men speak of justice they do not mean a sentimental condoning of guilt. When they talk about punishment they do not understand that evil-doers are to be applauded and petted. A prison is not intended, originally at least, to be the nearest approach we can make to Paradise. There is something better than pity for what is wrong; it is admiration for what is right. There is something higher than sympathy for sinners; it is worship for the good. There is something nobler than stooping down to guilt; it is the working up to an innocence that has no blemish and to a strength that has no flaw. There is a time for peace, and a time for war; a time for shedding tears, and a time for shedding blood; a time for feeding the poor and a time for flogging the garroter. A judge is the incarnation of justice, not the prototype of hysterical emotion. A weak judge is an enemy of the Commonweal. Mercy is meek. Justice is not at all meek, but stern, severe, rigid, with inexorable scale and remorseless sword. The brighter the splendour of mercy that waits for repentance with great-hearted and much-enduring gentleness, the deeper the shadow of justice that follows, shrouding the unrepentant in darkness and doom. When we speak of Infinite Mercy, we stand upon the furthest brink of kindness that we know, and still peer forth towards unending vistas of softened mysteries. When we would speak of Infinite Justice, we may say that it must be the utter and absolute cleaving asunder of right and wrong; but as we are silent with wonder at the abyss of reward above, so are we dumb with terror at the abyss of reprobation below.

Order is the end and the aim of the Universe. Order must be the motive power of all rational action, and the primal impulse of all dumb work. Intellectual creatures must harmonise means so as to gain the object that they wish; and physical forces must unite so as to produce the resultant outcome of some symmetrical effect. All this is only the vestige, the after-result, of the ordaining forces that are set in movement. But all this clearly shows that the first cause and final aim of Creation acts so as to produce order. The physical world is only useful, and therefore only good, in so far as it is a means for helping out the working of the moral world. Hence if order be of such paramount importance, as we see it to be, in the existence of material things, much more must order be desirable and of necessity to be attained, in that universe which is the highest and the noblest. Now, evil, moral evil, is disorder and discord. Moral evil outrages order in that region which is supreme. It cannot but be, that, if evil is possible, it should only be so, in as far as this permission of evil is only given that order may be more securely fixed at last. The permission of sin is only possible, on condition that sin be either repaired hereafter, or hereafter reduced by constraint to submit to order. Order must reign. Truth and Right must triumph in the end. Therefore, if not willingly, yet unwillingly, sin must submit. To every action there corresponds a reaction. If sin be willingly atoned for,

Mercy triumphs in the glory of Paradise regained. If sin be remorselessly adhered to, Justice must triumph in the warring down of the spirits that are for ever accursed as evil, because cursing good.

Our life moves on. Must it always move? Is there no term, no stay, no resting place, no home? While we journey through this life, we look forward with pilgrim eagerness, trusting that at length we may repose in peace for ever. It is deeply rooted in men's minds, and taught by every creed which purports to be divine, that after death shall come a life that is unchanged for evermore. While we live, we wait in trial; when we die, we face the everlasting recompense of good or ill. So men think. This much we may take as granted, that there may be a state of trial-time, and then a state of fixedness. Now, we only set this before your thought that during trial-time there must be hope of penitence, that yet life's trial-time may have a term wherein its lot is finally fixed. But, if there be a state of fixedness, there must be, for the soul that is fixed in evil, Hell.

Very few people have correct notions about the nature of Hell. Hence, it would be well worth our while to state what the teaching of Catholic Theologians is upon this matter. In order to avoid all possible suspicion of personal bias, I quote, from Fr. Christian Pesch, S.J., whose Work is recognized as a standard authority in Catholic schools of Theology. It will help to a fuller understanding of the suffering of the Lost, to consider in what precisely the beatitude of the Blessed consists. "In what beatitude or essential happiness consists is sufficiently indicated by the name of accidental Beatitude, which is such happiness as is not identified with essential happiness nor follows on it with an absolute necessity, but, while essential happiness exists, may or may not exist with it. Hence it is clear that the object of this accidental happiness is not the Vision of God; because whatever is included in the formal Vision of God, belongs to essential happiness." (Pesch Tractatus Dogmatici De Deo Fine Ultimo Vol. III. N. 473.) Now turn to consider the punishment of the Lost. "The punishment of the damned is twofold: The pain of loss, and the pain of sense. This twofold punishment of the damned is expressed in the words of the Judge. 'Depart from me into eternal fire' (Matt. 25. 41). The pain of loss is in the privation of the absolute Good.

It is said to be in a most special sense the pain of loss, for, although the pain of sense brings with it loss, yet this loss in comparison with the loss of the Beatific Vision is rightly esteemed as of no account. This pain of loss follows in a sort of natural way on mortal sin, because by his sin man turns away from God, and consequently God withdraws Himself from the man. The loss of essential beatitude brings with it the loss of accidental beatitude. Therefore in the damned there is not the light of infused faith, but another lesser knowledge is enough that by it they should be forced to recognise and avow the malice of their evil deeds . . . . which knowledge is sufficient that they should be tormented by their own conscience." (Pesch Vol. IX. N. 642.) "Therefore it will be a most extreme wretchedness for the damned that their intellect should be deprived completely of the Divine Light and that their will should be stubbornly set against the Divine Will; and this is the chief misery of the damned." (Suarez de Angelis Bk. 8. C. 6. N. 10.) Those students who wish to know the teaching of Catholic Theologians as to the nature of the fire which has been prepared for the "Devil and his Angels," will find the matter fully discussed in (Pesch Vol. IX. N. 653.) Consult also (Suarez De Angelis Bk. 8. C. 12. N. 9.) St. Thomas treats the question (Summa Contra Gentiles Bk. 4. ch. 90. p. 608) and (Sum. Theol. Q. LXX. A. III. p. 627). However, we need not speak of the "pain of sense" as Fr. Pesch and all other Theologians teach that "pain of sense" "is rightly esteemed as of no account in comparison with the pain of loss." It is of this latter that we speak. If a soul has wilfully fixed itself forever in guilt, and wilfully forever, holds relentlessly to guilt, such a soul cannot be loved by God, who can only love good, and the lovers of good. Such a soul is, then, lost to God. If such a soul knows its loss, it has the pain of loss. This is damnation. This is Hell.

Study for one moment the state of a soul that has left the clay which once was the living partner of its life. That soul while wedded to matter, thought through matter, and loved with matter. That soul when freed from what had in the beginning been the help, but what in the end had been the weight and load of clay, is now free to use its spiritual powers without fancy or feeling. Being spiritual, and being now thoroughly immaterial in its life, its intellectual vision is no longer abstract, because no longer dependent upon sense-knowledge but intuitive. It sees itself now through and through as it is. It comprehends itself thoroughly for there are no material clouds, no fantastic appearances, no hindrances of sense, to clog its action. It sees itself as thoroughly as it can be seen, and this without effort, without pause, without possibility of cessation. It is itself perfectly present to itself. It is, itself, purely intellectual as thinking subject, and it is, itself, purely intellectual as objective matter of thought. Wherefore, without need of further effort it is present to itself in thorough comprehension. Should such a soul during its years of trial, have warped and maimed its angelic powers, so as within itself to fix deep marks of wrong, so as of itself to make a hardened instrument of guilt; so as to transform its spiritual aspirations and highest tendencies into thought-out deliberate self-chaining bonds that tie it down to falsehood and to hate; then, of a truth, this soul is lost. Mark that this state may be brought about by one deliberate act of mortal sin; for, that deliberate act of mortal sin plunges the soul into the state of mortal sin. Indeed, this state may, in one moment, by a concentrated intensity of guilt, constitute a moral habit of the soul more satanic in its reprobate revolt than a long drawn series of sins which, while wilful and grave, were rather sins of weakness than sins of malice. Its substance now is spiritual and therefore changeless. Its intellect is now untrammelled and therefore comprehensive. Its will is now uninfluenced from without and therefore final. Its existence is all and all together, once and for ever, one substantial "*Now.*" It is in this "Now" of its own making, of its own choice, of its own keeping, an existence of hate, and therefore an existence of doom, and therefore a soul that God cannot love, and therefore a soul that God leaves to itself, and therefore a soul that is lost. It is in Hell. If there be pain when our material life is famishing for want of food, or when it is quivering from fever to fire, from fire to frenzy, in the delirium of thirst; if there be pain when a sharp sword cuts through palpitating flesh and shrinking nerve unto the very severance of body and of soul, must there not be pain, too, when the unimprisoned soul itself hungers with fierce want for such food as its nature needs, and, in the agony of a spirit, thirsts for Light and Love, while, yet, distempered with guilty gluttonness and befouled by evil aim, it cannot taste the good it touches, nor quench its uncontrollable anguish with the pure waters that ripple near?   Must there not be pain, when to its innermost depths, the soul is torn and tortured and rent asunder between its natural need and its acquired bent, between inborn yearning and encrusted habit, between spontaneous strivings towards good and wilful clinging to sin, between divine instincts that draw it upward with infinite attraction and accursed impulses, bred of its own malice, that drag it down with demon violence to the deathless suicide of a hating and hateful soul?

CHAPTER IV

FAITH

ALL men understand that, under certain conditions, they act reasonably when they accept as true, statements which are made by others with regard to matters which they do not themselves personally know. Those conditions are that, in the first place they know the speaker to be truthful, and that, in the second place they know the speaker to be well informed on the matter on which he speaks. Thus, Faith is the acceptance of truth on authority. Now, authority appeals to Faith and renders it reasonable through the evidence of its own knowledge and of its truthfulness. What is thus offered for belief is seen to be credible, and is therefore taken to be true. It is known to be worthy of belief, and therefore the admission of its truth is reasonable. Mark that in order to justify such acceptance of truth, there is no need of mathematical evidence nor even of the certainty of physical science. Moral certainty is quite enough, and moral certainty exists when the proof excludes all prudent doubt. Moral certainty in order to be real and sound need not render impossible a doubt that is imprudent. Divine Authority, by a metaphysical necessity, involves absolute knowledge and absolute truthfulness. But Divine Authority appeals not merely to the mind but also to the will. Of its very nature it involves a moral obligation. God's Word is not only worthy of belief, but furthermore it must be believed. Hence the steps towards Faith are these: — The mind recognizes that the grounds for belief are reasonable, and that there is a moral obligation to accept as true what God has declared to be true. Then, the will accepts that moral obligation, and moves the mind to make a further positive act of acceptance of the truth guaranteed by God's Authority. The reality of Revelation is shown sealed and sanctioned by divine signs. These divine signs are prophecies or works which are beyond the powers of nature or of man. These divine signs are evident, in a wide general way, to the world. In a special definite personal way, they may become evident to the individual man. One aspect will appeal to the student, another to the child. The most untutored savage of the wilderness or the most savage waif of the city may yet, through human testimony, receive such broad human reasons as shall enable him to receive the truth revealed by the Testimony which is Divine. For true and thorough Faith there is no need to be a Theologian. Indeed, amongst those who doubt, most only doubt because they do too much. They rush into extreme analysis, and get lost in a tangle of details. It were better far to turn their thought to a broad wide human appreciation of the Character, Life, and Work of Christ. Judging then by the ordinary standard of prudent common-sense in practical matters, they will recognise, in a plain simple way, that in Christianity there is something more than man could make, something that shows the Hand of God. In all this there must be the imperious appeal and the captivating winningness of Divine Grace; for Faith is a Gift of God. However, we are now speaking rather of human effort than of Divine Help. Thus, in one word the sensible, prudent, right thing to do is to accept the Word of God, revealed in and through the Christ, and, with one broad human submission to it as a whole to make our act of Faith.

CONCLUSION

Look up honestly towards the Light. Look up trustingly towards the Love of God. His Light and Love shine upon you and give warmth to your life. Live a true man's life. Recognise honourably what you know to be true. Do not grovel in the darkness, do not hide yourself in mist or shroud, do not say that you are dead; for there is a living life within you. Live a true man's life. See what all men see, the truth of God's Existence. Every ideal thought, every bounding aspiration, every throbbing impulse and every withdrawn sigh, every solid fact and every fairy dream, every impulse towards what is good and every shrinking back from wrong, every contact with physical fact and every reaching towards an unseen aim, every turn of everyday life and every epoch of your fate, every word of wisdom, every helping counsel, every warning uttered silently, every passing trifle and every constant care, whatever in your life is great or little, spiritual or material, vanishing or changeless, humorous or sad, all these things, pain or pleasure, grief or hope, life or death, all things speak to you of God. Recognise the truth. Live a true man's life. Live looking up and working up. Live like every man that was great and good. Live bowing down in adoration, reverence, and service before our Great God. Live looking up in trust, in hope, in love towards our Good God. Do not waste your trial-time in mad fancies. Do not waste your life in wild foolishness. Live a true man's life. Will you not do so? Then, poor weak blind doubting sinful child, kneel down and pray!